Also by Tammy Guest

Freedom from Fatigue: Naturally healing entrepreneurial burnout

*UN*RESTRICTED

a modern guide to
doing business and life *differently*

*UN*RESTRICTED

a modern guide to
doing business and life *differently*

TAMMY GUEST

the kind press

Cover design: Vari McKechnie
Editing: Georgia Jordan and Amy Molloy
Internal design: Nicola Matthews, Nikki Jane Design

Cataloguing-in-Publication entry is available from the National Library Australia.

NATIONAL
LIBRARY
OF AUSTRALIA

ISBN: 978-0-6450113-8-8
ISBN: 978-0-6450113-9-5 ebook

For all those feeling their souls being crushed
by ~~the~~ track changes and wriggly red underlines in
Microsoft Word.

And for showing up and sharing anyway.

Contents

Introduction

Once upon a time, I mentored a graduate naturopath. She was bright eyed and bushy tailed, and so insanely motivated and sure of herself that I couldn't possibly burst her bubble. Every time she visited the dispensary where she was working, she took a ginormous whiff of the herbs, as if she were drinking in water after days of dehydration.

She eyed the bottles with awe, mouthing the Latin names even though the regular names were all that appeared on the label. During the time between clients, she devoured clinical studies and textbooks to dive as deep as she dared into ways to help the people she served.

In her downtime, she obsessed over positioning the chair in the clinic to convey the right message, and fashioning her logo just right on her DIY website.

She would go home to her family hoping that her hard work was paying off and that all her efforts to realise this crazy dream wouldn't be for nothing. On tough days, she struggled with her inner critic and bouts of comparisonitis, plus the voice inside that said, *You should be spending more time with your family.*

She hoped, beyond anything, that she could show her kids that following your passion and helping people live healthy lives was noble and inspirational, even when times were challenging.

Many years later, the mentee started her own naturopathic practice. Her enthusiasm never wavered; she still had an unshakeable passion for natural health. She also had proof of the thousands of clients she directly helped and the thousands of practitioners who were ignited by her mission to improve the health of the planet.

She never lost her motivation for making things better, but she had thankfully lost a chunk of her ego, the chip on her shoulder and her frustration with the tough sides of her profession.

That mentee was me.

Twelve years after I started my first practice—a practice that would grow into a thriving business and a global entrepreneurial movement—I still have the same passion I had at the start. However, my mission has grown; I now look way beyond my own aspirations.

Today, I am more than a practitioner. I am a mentor, a speaker and a freedom seeker. I teach business owners how to live an *unrestricted life*—a life that blends work and life fluently, and allows you to think outside the box, tear up the rule book and redefine what success means for you.

As the founder of the Natupreneur Movement, it is my mission to amplify the value of practitioners so that they can create real change for their clients. But, this book—and my work—is not just for naturopaths.

I came up with the word natupreneur to talk about naturopaths who were building an empire, but it has become broader than that as I've worked with entrepreneurs across all industries.

To me, a natupreneur is someone who wants to build a business with an authentic, grounding and evolving ethos that supports the world and its healing. We can ALL be natupreneurs, and the planet and everyone on it needs us more than ever.

Today, health and business go hand in hand, no matter what industry you work in. As a business mentor, I help entrepreneurs worldwide to support themselves whilst building an empire, embrace change and activate change in their clients and customers.

Business as we know it has shifted and changed. Yet, too many businesses are being taught to operate as if they are frozen in time. What if we could see our work and our business as living, breathing organisms, with a heartbeat, that are forever evolving and growing, truly unrestricted?

What if we could learn to respect the passing of time and the seasons, and let ourselves rest as entrepreneurs, as well as thrive? What if we could 'grow with the flow' in our businesses? This is how you become a natupreneur—no matter what industry you work in.

As I wrap up the final edit of this book, I'm currently in a 'radical sabbatical'. A sabbatical is a fairly well-understood term in the world of academia; traditionally taken every seven years, this timeout consists of travel, writing and the pursuit of leisure. This affords the educator a new and fresh perspective with which to come back to their career.

I have been in my profession twelve years, so you could say my sabbatical was overdue. When I explore the timeline of my career in hindsight, that seven-year mark may have actually been the perfect time for a radical sabbatical ... but that's another story.

I sensed, for sure, that it was time for a sabbatical after running my largest, most complex event yet. In the break between waves of the pandemic, I brought together nearly three hundred participants across five different countries, both online and in person. When I look back, it was an extraordinary feat, myself, my virtual assistant and my on-the-ground event manager putting it all together.

In the lead-up, I could feel my edges beginning to fray. After years of cyclical biz burnout, I could sense something new wanting to come through me.

I have to make a distinction here: something wanting to come through is very different to chasing after the next thing, blowing something up and running away. It's also a very different energy to just staying where you are, ignoring the niggles and your intuition.

I didn't make a reactive, dramatic decision. I just looked at my business—and my life—and thought, how can I let it grow, evolve and bloom in this season of my life? For me, that meant giving myself room to transform again.

The gift of my sabbatical is exploring the space I can create in my life, getting curious about things that are important to me, and re-entering life with a fresh perspective.

Space is something I can see now and prioritise in my life. Space in my schedule, space in my office, space in my home, space in my mind. It has been so easy to fill my life up with stuff— having a full schedule of places to be, people to see, projects that need to be worked on now and no real space for the things I value the most, freedom and serendipity.

Space affords me an unrestricted life.

Pre-sabbatical, my calendar looked like a series of back-to-back meetings and to-do tasks. I would push through even if I was tired, I would put on a smiley face, I would 'do what it takes'. I would 'hustle'.

In New South Wales on the eastern coast of Australia, where I live, we are in our second major wave of the COVID-19 pandemic as I write this. It has irrevocably changed the face of business, health and travel globally. There has been a shift from the old masculine way of doing things to an acknowledgment of feminine leadership, flow, truth, lifestyle and business that supports us, rather than the other way around.

The pandemic, although challenging, has—much like my sabbatical—given many the gift of space; the opportunity to question what is true for each of us and re-enter the world with a fresh perspective. Whether this is in our business, relationships, profession, health, politics or spiritual beliefs, no stone has been left unturned in our examination of what's really important to us.

To be totally honest, the book I began to write last year was very different to the one in your hands. My original idea was a modern textbook of business for natural health practitioners, with a full bibliography, only available in university bookshops. This has thankfully morphed into a personal, heartfelt account of timeless tools that have helped me and my clients to navigate this crazy business life and the new world we find ourselves in.

Since the start of the pandemic, one of the deeper learnings I have come to understand, in business and in life, is the passing of time. The global slowdown has allowed for a true sense of time passing in its natural cycles.

As a practitioner, I have observed the menstrual cycle eventually give way to life.

As a hospital worker in my previous career, I perceived how the moon cycle gave way for the rise and fall of emotions in the emergency department. You'll notice the first four chapters of this book are themed around the four seasons—this is why! As a business owner, I was taught to focus on Q1 to Q4 (meaning the quarters of the fiscal year). The truth is, when we focus on the seasons and the energy they naturally flow into our business, we have a perfect system to guide our enterprise. Whenever I teach this at live events, I always have people coming up and asking, 'Why on earth has no one ever pointed this out before?'

This book is no longer just for naturopaths or anyone in a healing or therapeutic industry. Whether you work in the financial sector, at a tech startup, in a childcare centre, in retail or anything in between, you can feel vibrant, energised and alive in your job. It's not a feeling only yoga teachers, naturopaths and healers can achieve.

Perhaps you've come across this book at the very beginning of your business journey, or maybe you've been in business for a while and want to hit a new level. Regardless, it's time to expand the way your mindset and business work.

Each chapter in this book begins with a *brule*.

The Urban Dictionary defines a brule as:

> brule
> a bullshit rule,
> a rule we took on not through rational choice but
> through imitation, conditioning and many other
> different ways, a pattern we're all operating in.

Examples of brules could be:

- University education is necessary to have a decent career
- Every woman needs a man
- Nine-to-five is how work should be
- Religion is needed for salvation
- The pursuit of money is inherently bad

For almost every brule, there's a counter way of thinking. There are new studies, new research, new thinkers and new examples that show us these social rules are no longer true. The problem is, our brules can be very loud! They can be so incredibly ingrained in our beliefs that accepting a counterargument seems impossible— and that can restrict every aspect of our life.

The good news is, our brules can also become fuel. Whether you learned them from your well-meaning parents, your university lecturer who hadn't run a business, a friend in finance, or a best friend in a safe job, these social rules can be deconstructed into fuel that you can use for your business journey.

In this book, I share the brules I have bought into over the years and how I turned them into fuel. I'll also give you the tools to deconstruct your own brules and light your inner fire (get excited!).

My hope for you, in reading this book, is that you can keep what feels right for you and get curious about what might not be serving you. Let go of the competition, frustration, comparison and obsession with more knowledge—and invite in the possibility that everything you need is inside you already; you just need to lean in and take it.

By our final chapter together, you will have a new set of skills—skills you can keep coming back to whenever you need to refresh or progress to the next level of your work life. Together, we'll also prune the limiting beliefs that are holding you back to boost your confidence, self-belief and imagination.

My hope for you is that you can use the tools in this book to create space; get curious about the brules holding you back and what you might choose instead; and finally re-enter life with a fresh perspective.

Writing this book has been the perfect example of the power of an unrestricted mindset. In allowing myself the space and freedom to let this book evolve, the result has morphed and changed through the seasons of the pandemic. If I had become stuck in my mindset of what this book 'should' include for a pre-pandemic world, this book wouldn't be everything it needs to be for right now.

You don't need to take a sabbatical to have an unrestricted work life. You can find it every day as you still tick off your commitments, care for your family—and yourself—and allow your business and your dreams to keep growing.

So, take a breath, loosen your shoulders, feel the excitement in your stomach and the expansion in your heart.

It's time to let your restrictions go.

Tammy x

How to read this book

Bhule: Entrepreneurship is all go, all the time

Fuel: There is a reason and a season for all of it; follow the flow

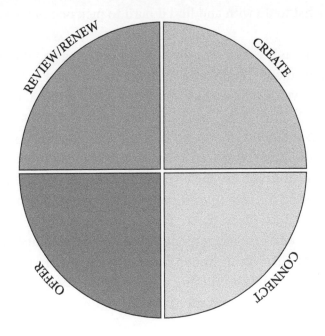

The Cycle of Entrepreneurship (pictured above) has been a guiding map of mine for some time now. Over the years, it has grown in depth and layers as I rediscovered the phases of the moon and the cycles of the seasons.

The more I follow this cycle and the more I share it with my mentees, the more flow appears in our lives and businesses. You will notice it also guides the content of this book, with each chapter fitting into one of the stages.

If we take a look at each section of the cycle and consider it like a clock face, we begin at midnight and the CREATE section of our enterprise, followed by CONNECT at three, OFFER at six, then REVIEW/RENEW at nine.

Create is the time in our cycle where ideas are formed and we create something from nothing. Create is the spark of insight that comes to dance with us. Often business owners that feel at home in the Create zone are makers; they have more ideas than they know what to do with and find it hard to pick one to take action on.

Create has the corresponding season of spring and the essence of the new moon. It is the energy of the bud of a new seeding, and the first sliver of light as the moon makes its way into a new cycle.

Connect is finding the words and pictures to clearly bring an idea to the people who need and want it. It begins with messaging and marketing, but also includes finding the right people to work with to bring the idea to fruition. Without people, the best ideas remain just that: ideas.

Connect has the corresponding season of summer and the essence of the waxing moon. It is the energy of spreading a message like wildfire, shining a light on the idea, and gaining momentum as the moon speeds to full.

Offer is the exchange of value; putting a price on the idea and collecting money for it. It is taking people and converting them into paying customers, and then redistributing the funds wisely to ensure flow continues. Without this exchange, the enterprise stops. This also encompasses the platforms on which we house our offering, and the payment gateways, accessibility methods, and automation we use to create a nurturing exchange.

Offer's corresponding season is autumn, with products being sent out into the world and becoming fuel for the next cycle—much like fallen leaves. Its essence is the full moon phase, representing the fullest expression of an idea shared.

Review/Renew is the time of the cycle that so many entrepreneurs miss or skip over; it is the time to regroup, restore our energy, and reassess with a clear mind what worked, what didn't and what could be done better next cycle. The restoration of ourselves and our cells is vital for longevity in business. The review process creates opportunities to see where time, energy and money might be being wasted, or where there are gaps that can be filled by our unique skills, talents, products and offerings. New ideas can be born from a clear perspective here.

Review/Renew has the corresponding season of winter, the energy of going inward, and the essence of the waning moon as the light fades to create the fresh slate of the new moon.

This doesn't mean you can only implement these strategies during certain seasons of the year—it is simply a guide. What I would love you to realise is that everything is cyclic. When you are beating yourself up for not achieving enough or not feeling in a hustle mindset, realise that this is perfectly natural and it makes your business more sustainable. Every stage is valid and equally important.

Although this cycle may not follow the timeframes of the seasons or the phases of the moon per se, it could. The value of it lies in the peace and ease of knowing that the flow of our business takes on a similar rhythm to these cycles we see in nature, and that when we work with this rhythm rather than against it, organic growth can occur. This principle forms the core of natupreneurship.

You will find a deeper dive in the coming chapters into the nuances of each part of the cycle of entrepreneurship, as well as some tools and wisdom that I've found helpful along the way. For now, remember, there is a reason and a season for it all—follow the flow.

Chapter 1
Create

Rule: Make it up as you go along

Fuel: Failing to plan is planning to fail

I'll never forget taking one of our many mastermind retreats to Bali—we had an incredible bunch of business owners ready to rise to the next level by taking time out of their business to work on it, rather than in it.

It was a sultry South-East Asian morning; the smell of incense hung in the air and a haze across the rice paddy fields obscured the famous volcano Mount Agung from view. We waited in the reception of our hotel for the minibus to take us on the day's excursion high into the mountains of Ubud. The nervous chatter of the group was occasionally muffled by water running into the nearby lily pond.

When I run retreats, I like to facilitate experiences that will enable our attendees to truly understand a concept. This was day three of the retreat, so everyone was getting used to one another and the chatter continued on the bus during the hour-long drive into the mountains.

Soon enough, we all bundled out of the bus onto a nondescript road in an area known by the locals for all the silversmiths who work there. Similarly, there are regions for carpenters, window makers, and glassblowers—seemingly whole suburbs snaking up the mountains, dedicated to one craft or another.

I had brought everyone here, to a silversmith shop, to create their own silver piece to take home. We sat with Made, the elderly owner of the little carport workshop, who was there as our guide. As he handed out raw lumps of silver, we expected to have a step-by-step demonstration.

Instead, he sat back in his chair and asked, 'Okay, what do you want to make?'

I wish you could have seen the look on our faces. I hadn't realised that this seemingly simple question could be the cause of so much angst.

What *did* we want to make? If we could make … anything!

For these business owners, including me, the idea of creating without restrictions was alien but also exhilarating.

For the next two hours, our group went on a mission to seek our inspiration. We poured over finished pieces in the silversmiths. We went back into the shop to look for ideas. We discussed it with one another at length: the pros and cons, level of difficulty, sureness of success, and length of time to complete a piece.

We only had four hours there and most of it was taken up by the quandary of finding our vision. The options were limitless and that was the problem—everyone wanted to create something great, but what did that look like?

Many of us eventually settled on small, simple rings or bars with stamped letters or inspiring words. One incredible attendee, however, did something different. She created an amazing dachshund-shaped piece of art to wear as a necklace. Although her idea took more time and unique skills, the clarity of her vision allowed her to find the right people from Made's family to help her. She didn't waste time comparing and contrasting.

Every business owner—hell, every human—wants to create a life they are proud of, but when we are given a blank slate and we have all the ideas, or are stunned into having none, one of the most powerful questions to answer is, *What do you want to create?*

The more clarity you have in answering this, the more ease you will have in finding the resources, people and time to forge your creation.

In this chapter, we explore the four main areas you will come back to time and time again to turn your ideas into reality:

- **Why?** Your flight plan.
- **Who?** Your ideal client.
- **What?** Your business model.
- **How?** Your new offerings.

Your flight plan

Rule: We are entrepreneurs; we can wing it

Fuel: Knowing where you are going is the first step to getting there

Just like in any journey, you always need to know where you're going in order to get there. You pop an address into your GPS and off you go. Did I mention that I'm also a helicopter pilot? When I fly helicopters, it is the same concept—there's no way I'm just going to take off and not know which direction I'm headed.

This also applies to your business: without a clear direction or a specific plan, you're not going to know how to get to your desired location.

So, let's talk about our flight plan. We need to have a vision of how to get there, even if we have never flown this path before. Our plan can also keep us on track when unexpected things happen, giving us an opportunity to course correct or ignore bright, shiny objects that take our attention away from the path in front of us.

I want you to grab a pen and paper and jump into the future.

Go through each area of your life and create your new future using the writing prompts below. We need to take the time to get clear now, because the clearer we are on our path, the easier it is for the brain to believe this is happening. Anything that you have written down today in your flight plan, you can create a forward vision for.

Your ideal day
- What would your ideal day look like? Write it out in detail.
- How much money would you be earning, or already have in the bank?
- What is the figure that you feel comfortable with achieving, but also may be a bit of a stretch? It doesn't have to be a million dollars or a seven-figure business. It all depends on you and where you're at.

Now, on to your personal wellbeing
- What do you look and feel like?
- Do you dress in a certain way?
- Do you have a certain style?

Your reputation
- How do people talk about you?
- What does it look like when you stand up on stage?
- What are you well known for?

Then your business
- How does your business look and feel?
- What are the things that you have achieved over the past year in your business that you are proud to write down?
- How many people have you helped?
- How many people have you helped through online courses or other online contributions?
- What type of customers do you have?
- Who are your favourite customers?
- Do you have a fair relationship with partners in business?

What about your team?
- Who is in your team? Have you hired a virtual assistant, employee, personal assistant, clinic manager, or marketing coach?
- What have you done this year that has created an opportunity for you to not be alone in this? What things have you outsourced that were out of your zone of genius?

In your body
- What personal health practices have you been using this year?
- How do they feel inside your body?
- How did you treat this body of yours over the past year?

Your home
- What exactly does your home look like?
- Have you moved house? Are you working from home?
- Have you made any changes when it comes to your business?

- Are you able to run your business while you're away?
- Have you changed anything about your home to be more innovative?

Your family
- What are your relationships like? What do they look like?
- What does it look like to spend time with your partner, the children?
- Are you happy with the friends that you have? Are they inspiring to you?
- Are your friends cheerleaders and advocates for what you do?
- Are your friends challenging you in a way that helps you grow?

Your network
- How many people did you meet this year who challenged you and helped you grow?
- What are their names?
- How did you connect with them?

Your mentors
- Who has crossed your path that allows you to stay two steps ahead?
- What type of relationship do you have with them?

Your travels
- What areas of the globe have you been to?
- Where are you looking forward to going?
- What are your reasons for travel? Is it for fun? For clients? Business retreats?

How about your hobbies outside of work, or outside of the home?
- What are the things that came through this year? Maybe you're connected to your creator in an artistic way; maybe you got a lot more active; maybe something came about that took you outside so you're no longer inside all the time.
- What are your new hobbies or your new skills?

Your time
- How do you manage your time? What does that look like?
- How does your schedule support your boundaries and help you to stay in control?
- How do you spend your time? How have you invested your time?

Your peace of mind
- Do you feel that you have peace of mind?
- Are you worried and overwhelmed?
- Are you creating a space to look after yourself at your current pace?
- What does your mindset look like now?
- What do you love about your life?
- What mindset do you aspire to?

Your sense of purpose
- What does your sense of purpose look like? Are you contributing and giving back to your community and/ or the world? If so, in what way? How does it feel to be aligned with your purpose?
- What are your plans for the future? What's coming up in the next year?

Your ideal client

Bhule: I can help everyone

Fuel: My gifts and talents are for unique people out there who need my uniqueness

It is really important to take some time out to connect with the person that you are here to help. It changes absolutely everything about your business when you know who you are truly here to serve. We are often told not to become too niche! I know the stories you're telling yourself. *What if I choose that person and nobody else comes? I'm just starting out and I really want to see everybody; what's wrong with being a generalist?*

Of course, there's nothing wrong with being a generalist IF your product or service naturally fits the entire population. But, that is rarely true. More often, we have a product or service that can support, ignite and elevate a portion of the population. Instead of accepting and embracing that, we waste time and energy trying to package our product or service up in a way that appeals to all—diluting our value in the process.

The questions I'm asked all the time are, *What should my message be? What should my marketing be? How do I actually get to the people out there that need my help?*

This all comes down to your ideal client.

I want you to really get to know your ideal client; meet them in your imagination, wake up with them in your mind and feel the difference you can make to their life experience.

Exercise
Step into the world of your ideal client

Tammy Guest

Let's create magic together

In the top section of the pictured work sheet, write out the motivations your ideal client has, what could bring them heartbreak and what's actually causing them pain emotionally. What is the problem you are helping to solve? Is it physical, mental, emotional? If so place it in its corresponding area of the person in the image. In the body section, if you specialise in different areas of the body, different conditions or symptomatology, then pop them in.

Consider what they are thinking about, what they aspire to and what they perspire over—what are the things that keep them up in the middle of the night? Underneath, you'll see a rectangular section all about what they stand for and what they want.

We'd also need to consider the things that can't

budge in their life. My ideal client used to be a busy mum. She would find her way to me through a bootcamp referral or from other practitioners, or maybe through Facebook groups or word-of-mouth. She would come in presenting with physical symptoms: fatigue, and perhaps a little bit of anxiety. She would talk about aspiring to go on a meditation retreat, knowing she would never commit to it at this stage in her life.

Knowing your clients is about realising their desires and their dreams, but also their limitations. Knowing your client helps you make your service achievable for and relatable to them.

For me, at that point in my practise, it was about thinking:

If I were to create a workshop or an event for her on a Saturday morning, there is no way she would show up for it, because her kids come first.

If she can't commit to a long weekend retreat, how can I offer a miniature version of this service?

How can I help her to get over her guilt that she's treating herself, and realise that she deserves to prioritise her health?

For every niche, this will be different, but it's all about getting to know your client—intimately. What are the blocks your particular client has that you need to overcome before you even get there? How can you address the blocks between you and them?

The next question is, *How do I meet them?*

Once you've filled out the work sheet and taken the time to really consider where your ideal client is at, then consider where they've come from.

- *Are they coming from a specialist?*
- *Are they coming from Facebook groups?*
- *What are they interested in?*
- *Where do they hang out (either digitally or offline)?*
- *Did they talk to other people to eventually find you as their health practitioner?*
- *What has been coming up for them in their body, mind and spirit?*

This information is gold because it allows you to create your message and your marketing, adjust the copy on your website, fill out your Facebook page or even create a group that's specifically for these people.

What about everyone else?

This is the question that I get the most whenever I explain the power of client focus. *If I just have my ideal clients and all my focus is on them, what happens to everyone else? What if they all want to come and see me?*

Well, they'll continue to come and see you regardless. It's a bit like having a spotlight on one particular person, but there's always ambience around. If you're spotlighting that one mum who's standing out the front of the school, then all of the mums standing with her, all of her work friends and even her family members will very likely want to come and see you as well.

Don't forget that it makes your life easier to get your ideal client *and* know that you are still going to help so many other people as well.

Your business model

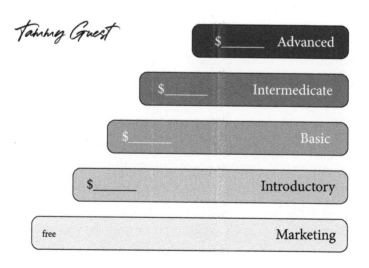

Bhule: Business is the same for everyone; work hard and you'll succeed

Fuel: Building a business is unique to you, your progress and your potential clients' journey

Alright, how are you going to create a new program, product or offering so that you can help your ideal client? What is your process when it comes to determining what is a good idea over one that could waste time, effort, energy and money?

Well, if you have a solid business model that you're in alignment with, it can make this step so much easier.

In the example business model pictured, you'll see that there are multiple tiers in your business. In this section, you'll find the steps that your ideal client is going to take on their journey of utilising *your* business.

Tammy Guest

$_____ Advanced

$_____ Intermedicate

$_____ Basic

$_____ Introductory

free Marketing

At the base of this pyramid, you're going to be creating a whole bunch of free content. This is so people can connect with you, either online or offline, and get little chunks of information that will make them interested in the next thing. For some of you, it might be social media; for others, it might be presenting to your local community.

The next step is where these same people can pay you a small amount of money for the information you provide. For a lot of business owners, this could be a book (print or digital)—this way people can get a real taste of what you're actually all about.

Following on from that, the next step for most practitioners, consultants or coaches is your one-on-one consultations. In the beginning, it is usually a one-on-one consultation and a follow-up. If you think back to your ideal client and put yourself in their shoes, is a one-on-one consultation and follow-up truly what they need to move forward? If your answer is no, then what else could you provide them?

Think about what might move them forward; they might pay a little bit more money for it, but it will actually be the best thing for their journey. Perhaps a better alternative for your ideal clients could be the offer of programs and packages.

Come back to who your client is and the barriers they might have to progressing—time, money, guilt, priorities. This could help you to decide the best next step, whether it's a multi-session package, an online component, maybe a small e-course or a one-off masterclass.

Our business plans are really about taking our client on a journey—from our first point of contact to their ultimate end goal. The good news is there are many ways to achieve this!

Your new offerings

Rule: Just keep offering something new

Fuel: Where your gifts and talents meet the needs and desires of clients, magic happens

I like to call your services or products 'offerings', because that is exactly what they are. It's not the next trend that you are selling clients; it's an offering. Every business will have different offerings to suit its owner's skill set and capabilities, and its clients' desires and preferences. This is where it gets exciting because there really is no limit—it's all about picking and choosing the best fit for you and your clients.

Masterclasses can help accelerate your client's understanding of the concerns or challenges relevant to them. Supporting them through a deep dive into this kind of 'homework' not only empowers your client but frees up the time you might have otherwise spent with them in one-on-one consultations. You might consider publishing the program as a combination of e-courses and ebooks, specifically for different types of people who come and see you. Think detox, cleanse and gut health packages, and even reproductive and fertility packages.

Your business should have an ultimate offering: your **master product or service**—the one you're so very proud of, whose price point you're totally confident in. This is where you can let your imagination run wild. This could be a premium-priced retreat, or whatever gets your juices flowing.

It's an extraordinary experience to run a business; you really have to take the time to envisage what this journey can look like not only for your clients, but for yourself as well.

When you're thinking about your offerings, a brainstorming session is a great place to start.

1. Consider and write down what offerings are actually in alignment with you and your business at this point in your life.
When I had babies, that season of my life was quite time poor. It was difficult to get on client calls and consults, but I could create a number of articles on my phone or laptop and offer them together as an emailed course.

The season of my life when I cared for my mum after surgery for breast cancer afforded me plenty of time to run group programs and calls from my phone.

You get to choose what your business looks like in this season of your life.

2. Explore what your client wants.
If you really took a deep dive and spent some time connecting with your clients, you'll know what they want. You'll know what their aspirations are. You'll know their challenges and you'll know what they would love in their life to take the next step on their journey.

And if you completed your business model exercise, you'll understand what's the next logical step to take your client on.

3. Is your offering in alignment with YOU?
Consider whether your offering is in alignment with your flight plan. What do you personally want out of life? How can you create offerings that support this, either through financial gains or freedom?

Don't commit to something that will end up costing you too much time or money, or make you feel stuck. The sweet spot where your needs for this season of life and your clients' wants intersect is where a great offering begins.

4. Narrow it down!

Sometimes, we have too many great ideas and not enough time in the day to action them. It's important to invest our energy in the ideas that really fit with our purpose, otherwise we'll feel untethered and ungrounded, constantly chasing after new shiny objects.

Have you heard of the Japanese concept ikigai? Ikigai is waking up in the morning to do something on purpose. It can help with choosing the right idea for an offering that not only fills up your cup, but also fills the cup of your target market.

Answer these four questions, either in your journal or aloud:

1. What do you love to talk about?
2. What do you love getting into a conversation about that makes time fly? (Often this will happen when we are seeing clients in the clinic, and all of a sudden sixty minutes disappear because we've been so into what we want to share).
3. What information, that you can share, will people pay for?
4. What are you good at?

Question four can be hard to answer ourselves, after years of being told not to boast (especially as women!). It's time we all became more comfortable with our talents, especially if we want our clients to benefit from them.

What do you have a particular flair for?

If you hit a brick wall, ask friends or colleagues what they think you are good at. I've done this exercise, and I can tell you it's very revealing! When I posed the question to my social media followers, I got a whole variety of answers. The answer that came up most frequently, though, was my ability to provide answers to large, complex questions and explain them in an easy-to-understand way.

So, what am I good at? I'm able to explain things clearly.

Finally, ask yourself: what does the world need?

There is a Disney movie called *Robots* where they explore the concept of 'see a need, fill a need'.

When I had my clinic, I knew I was good at helping stressed-out mums with their adrenal fatigue. I got paid for this and I could explain the biochemistry behind it really well—inspiring others in their lifestyle choices. I loved the aha moments that these women had when sitting across from me. I wrote a book that detailed my own story of adrenal fatigue. This ticked all the ikigai boxes.

In the case of my latest offering, this book, the need that I saw was to link natural health and business together—and here we are!

Making the time

In all this self-evaluation, you may see some discrepancies between how you have been spending your time and what you've envisioned in your flight plan. The tasks you're filling your day up with may not actually be moving the needle or helping you to execute your flight plan.

Your next task is to create the time you want.

- Write down how you invest time into your priorities.
- Now add in your family time, your self-care time, your client-facing time, and the time you spend working on your business and its needs.

- Write down where you create time and space to get yourself closer to your flight plan.

Now, if your flight plan has an ideal number of clients you want to serve, you may need to review how much time you actually have to see clients and incrementally increase this. For example, if you're currently seeing two clients per week and your goal is twenty, then maybe create a goal of seeing ten clients per week within six months. So, how can your weekly time schedule facilitate this?

If you are worried about social media being a time suck, then it can be handy to create before you consume—especially if you're using social media as part of your business strategy. We also need to look at it from both a money and time perspective. You want the time you *invest in* to be *paying off* financially. So, if you're investing an hour on social media and you currently charge $100 per hour to see clients, then for that hour invested in social media you should be generating $100 online.

Invest your time wisely

When you create the time to do marketing, you want to make sure you're getting a return on that investment of time. So you want to be creating something that can come back to you—like an offer or an opportunity for a new client to join you. Be honest with yourself regarding the return on investment that you want for your marketing time, because you can't get that time back.

Make sure that you're also honouring the parts of your flight path that contain your core values. Invest your time in your family, in getting out in nature, in your hobbies—because creating the days that you want leads to the weeks, months and years that you want to truly live.

Investing time to save time

Rule: There's never enough time

Fuel: Time is what we make it

It's a fresh, new week and you can't wait to get stuck into it because there's a long to-do list in your head. But all of a sudden, it's mid-morning on the Friday and you haven't been able to get all the things done, all the things you had committed to. Where did your week go?

We all have twenty-four hours in a day—the difference is in *how* we invest or spend that time.

It's similar to the concept of spending or investing money. We can invest in a good-quality car upfront that's going to give us longevity and save us money in the long run, or we can spend money on an older bomb, never to get the money back. Generally, we'll find that we will need to spend money on the older car more often than if we had just invested smartly in the first place. It is the same with time.

So, where are you spending your time? How can you invest your time smartly so you gain more longevity in the long run?

In business, you need to invest your time in things that will give you back more time in the future. You may invest your time in creating a program and then invest your time in launching it, but it will be servicing your clients in the long run with minimal time expenditure on your part. So, even though you're investing time upfront, you're saving it later. You can then spend that saved time with the kids, or go on holidays. But you need to make that front-end investment first.

Action

Create a time tracker

Write down how you spend your time each day for three days. Go all-in on this, and no cheating! Don't write down a glorified version of your days or what you think looks good; it will be really tempting to do this, but don't.

Literally track your time in fifteen-minute increments. This way, you start seeing patterns, or where you prioritise certain things.

I dare you to start doing it now, not just in your mind; the impact comes from writing it out.

"

Failing to plan
is planning to
fail.

Chapter 2
Connect, Communicate

 **Bhule:** Paying for ads is the new way to get leads

Fuel: The gold standard for connection is still word-of-mouth, but it's all about how you do it

For me, one of the most important pillars in living an unrestricted life is connection—connection to yourself, of course, but also connection to the people you can help and the people who can amplify your message.

When I first worked with a business coach, I was told to get referral partners, meet quotas in networking, and a whole bunch of other things that just didn't sit well with me.

What I actually found is it's really about connection, and nurturing those connections in alignment with you and your values. Without this, people's bullshit detectors go off. You've probably felt it: when you read someone's Instagram post and you just can't quite buy it. It feels salesy and stilted, and not in line with their character.

It's not easy to make and maintain aligned connections in your business, but it is worth it, I promise you. Whether it's connecting authentically with your clients, your social media followers or other people in your industry, making aligned connections is the key to growing and evolving your work—and never having to feel alone.

In this chapter, I'm asking you to emotionally invest time and space into your marketing and your message. If this is the first time you've come across these concepts, then it's the perfect time to really understand your marketing and branding, and how your message is getting to your ideal client.

If you're further down the business path, maybe it's time to revisit your message and the avenues you're using to connect. We are going to explore marketing and branding in a new way, and really get to the essence of your messaging so that it's consistent across both online and offline spaces.

We will also look at collaboration and how the universal law of reciprocity can really come in handy when it comes to connecting with the people who are totally in alignment with you and your business. This is about forming connections that yield real results and also bring you the social energy we all need to shine.

Referrals without the cringe

Bhule: I seem pushy if I ask my clients to tell their friends about my offerings

Fuel: My clients' friends could be praying for a service like mine

The first step in getting word-of-mouth referrals is servicing the person right in front of you. Referral-based business models are all about a chain reaction. You help someone who can't wait to tell their friends, and so on. It's not a passive strategy for business owners, however: you can play a part in pushing the message onwards.

If a client has come to you more than once, it's because they've received some benefit from you. They are using more of their precious time to come see you again because they have found value in what you are giving. And if they find value in your offering, it's very likely they know somebody just like themselves who will find value in it as well.

If they happen to know someone who needs the same kind of benefit, you're actually doing a disservice to everyone who doesn't know you exist yet if you hold back and say nothing.

In my naturopathic business, I was always aware that there were umpteen people with chronic conditions out there: people getting sicker and sicker every day. If I encouraged my clients to recommend me to their friends, I was opening up opportunities for their friends to heal faster. It's all about having confidence in your product or your service, and your role on the planet.

So, how can you encourage referrals without making it awkward? Instead of staying quiet, or hoping, or manifesting them talking to somebody else, it's as simple as having a conversation.

Start the conversation with something like this:

> 'Hey, isn't it amazing what we've done in such a short period of time? For you to go from here to here.'

Reference the goals they've achieved through working with you— they might have lost a couple of kilos or doubled their amount of energy. Review their follow-up sheets for the measurements you've registered. For instance, when they first came to you, they were a 2 out of 10 for sleep or energy and now, only X amount of time later, they're an 8 out of 10.

Don't say:

> 'I'm a referral-based business. Can you please give
> me referrals? Here are my business cards.'

Isn't that icky? It's kind of weird and not a conversation you want
to be in.

A conversation where you are applauding the work someone
else has done for themselves is another story. Because it's not up
to us to fix somebody—it's up to them to take their journey. It's
their choice to take that medicine, make those lifestyle choices.
So applaud them for what they've done.

If you really like working with a particular client, it's very likely
you're going to enjoy working with their friends. Suggest that if
anyone else in their life has similar stuff going on and would love
to feel better, they can come see you.

> 'I really want to help more people just like you. If you
> know someone who could do with the same kind of
> help, if you feel at all moved, please give them my
> card. Feel free to let them know I'm here and what
> we've done.'

'What we've done together' is a very different conversation.
It's inviting them to tell their story. Having the opportunity to
celebrate your health is such a cool thing for anyone who has lost
or gained weight or done anything specifically for their health
and benefitted from it.

So that's how to have a conversation to help more people.

Bonding with other businesses

Bhule: I can't work with them; they're my competition

Fuel: Collaboration over competition is where community thrives

I run a challenge for my mentees to go and introduce themselves to local businesses—businesses who can potentially refer clients to them. In the naturopathic field, this would be doctor's clinics or other health-based businesses such as local gyms. In your field of work, it would be any local business that is aligned with your work—a business that doesn't offer your exact service, but whose clients could benefit from your skill set.

Whenever I encourage my mentees to do this, they have the same hurdle; why would this business help me? They've got enough to do, advertising their own services!

This is where I want you to totally flip your mindset. Why *wouldn't* they want to offer their clients another service, if it doesn't take away from their own business? No business can be everything to everyone. Isn't it great that they have another avenue to direct customers down, if they can't personally serve them?

Here are some examples of potential partnerships:

- A bootcamp for mums and a casual childcare service
- A coffee shop inhabited by many entrepreneurs and a local coworking space
- A coworking space and a tech repair service
- A library and a book writing course
- A real estate agent and an interior styling service
- A spa and a nutritionist consultant

- A wedding dress retailer and a wedding venue

The list is endless.

When we start to think about local businesses, our inner critic can come into play. What if they don't like my service or agree with what I offer? This is a big hurdle for naturopaths approaching doctor's surgeries. Personally, I had a brule that 'all doctors think naturopaths are quacks'. I had to work to change that brule into fuel: it takes a village to help people to heal. Every service can offer different benefits to different people.

In actual fact, one of my favourite referrers was a general practitioner. Multiple specialists referred patients to me and this continues to be the case with many practitioners.

After working with thousands of practitioners who had their best referrals from doctors, or even worked in integrative medical practices, I know this isn't an anomaly.

How do we get to know one another?

When it comes to connecting with other businesses, sending an email probably isn't going to cut it. Instead, we can introduce ourselves. If you're a naturopath or similar, you have to actually show up to the practice and speak to the practice manager.

The practice manager is usually extremely busy and pressed for time. Being able to connect with them in a quick and easy manner is key. You need to be able to say, quite easily and quickly, *Hey, this is who I am, this is where I am. Here is something I would love to be able to help the practice with. I'd love to be able to meet with the doctors, and here is more about me.*

Then it's up to you to ask if the practice has a 'Lunch and Learn', or a weekly staff meeting. Is there a time you can visit most of the doctors at the same time, to help their clients? The goal is NOT for you to get referrals. It's about *helping the clients of the practice.*

This can be applied to any business setting, from small business to corporate. The old adage 'It's not what you know; it's who you know' rings true here. The more personal the connection, the more the relationship has a chance to thrive.

Although the gold standard is a face-to-face meeting, the world we live in now has created a great opportunity to connect online or over the phone. As easy as it seems to just cold email or direct message a potential connection, it is always preferable to organise a meeting so you can see or hear one another for true human-to-human contact.

Think about the kind of businesses you could partner up with. How could it be a reciprocal arrangement? What could you offer the business's customers or clients that would pair perfectly with what they are offering? Reach out to them with a generous heart and a real desire to help people. The perfect partnerships and business recommendations feel authentic and not forced, and genuinely offer the client or customer something unique or different.

The fantastic bit is the follow-up

Don't be the person who strikes up a new connection with a business, then ghosts them. The follow-up is where the magic happens. The follow-up is where it's at.

Okay, so you've gone into a business in person, handed over your card and, casually, talked about arranging a time to talk further. Let's face it: you're probably not the top priority of whoever you spoke to. That's okay! The ball can be in your court for a follow-up. This is when it's fine to send that email:

Hey, it was so wonderful to meet you the other day. I love the practice. I got online and did some research, and you're the only practice in the area that does [whatever their specialty is].

You are starting a conversation, just as you would with a new friend, instead of putting your business hat on and doing the business thing, then coming across as weird and asking for referrals.

Your email might say:

Oh my goodness, I can't believe you do [whatever their speciality is]. I'm so excited about it. I actually have similar clients. I'd love to help the people that come to you. These are the types of things I do: [your offerings]. Can I come in and have a chat?

The same goes for catching up with another business owner or colleague at a conference or networking event—the fantastic bit is in the follow-up. Consider how many people you meet at these events, or how many proposals to work in collaboration come across a desk weekly. Then consider how many people hand their card over or introduce themselves in passing, never to be heard from again?

The way to stand out—from the heart, with genuine care—is to be fantastic in the follow-up.

Not everyone will like you!

Rule: I have to be general so that I don't alienate customers or potential partners

Fuel: Focusing on the people who align with me helps everyone

This is something I learnt about three years into my practice: your vibes will not match with everybody's ... and that is totally okay!

When you embrace your niche as a practitioner, consultant or coach, potential referrers—and people who need the kind of help that you specialise in—will usually be keen to work with you. Those who are way out of your niche will more than likely find someone else to work with. And that's okay too.

The fear factor

Rule: If I feel nervous, it means I don't believe in my product

Fuel: Nerves are a sign I really love what I do and that I care

You don't get these opportunities to connect if you don't step up and make friends with the fear. I know it can be especially nerve-racking if you're presenting to a group, either in real life or virtually. We all know when people are not totally engaged in our presentation, especially on Zoom if they're typing as you're talking (we've all been there!).

Remember, if there are nine people in that room, four of them are probably madly writing up reports and trying to keep up with all of their work. They might not be a hundred per cent listening to you. Don't get offended if they're not.

But even if they have a million other things to do, what might stand out for them is the story you told about the really tough client or case that you were able to turn around using your knowledge and skill.

Whatever it is that stands out for them, when they next see someone just like that, they're going to remember you and maybe say:

> 'Hmm, well I can give you this for now, but it would be great if you went to see the consultant/clinician/ coach down the road.'

Go ahead, feel the fear; lean in and have the conversation anyway. Don't get offended if they don't respond with the same energy; don't take it personally, because it's not about you. There is so much going on in medical practices, small businesses and big companies that you don't see in an everyday situation. If there's one person in the room who sends you one extra client, guess what? You've helped one extra person that you wouldn't have helped otherwise.

It's not about the referral. It's not about you winning or failing at this conversation. It's being able to help that one person who wasn't going to get help the way you can give it. That one person who wasn't going to gain access to the natural health information that you have.

Because you stepped up and felt the fear and had the conversation anyway, you helped that person.

I love this idea so much; it always gives me goosebumps thinking about it. If you, reading this, could have just one extra conversation—one you didn't think you could—and it turns into one extra person being helped, that has an incredible ripple effect. You just never know what could happen from that.

If they were to tell another person about their experience, that's twice the amount of people who could get help—just by you being brave enough to stand in front of a potential partner and talk with them for three seconds.

For me, when I was building my naturopathic practice, those three seconds became enjoyable instead of scary. It looked like standing in front of a health practitioner and saying (something like):

> 'I'd like to bring some blueberry muffins and have a conversation; I'd love to find out who I can refer to your medical practice.'

It's all about feeling the fear, doing it anyway and then being able to help somebody. Don't get yourself tripped up on the idea that it has to be perfect. Not everyone is going to like you. Not everyone is going to like blueberry muffins!

You are going to fumble at first. Don't get yourself all worked up that not everybody in the room is going to love you. Focus on the one that does, and don't get scared of the word referral. It's literally a conversation to help somebody more than you would have before.

Challenge
Just one conversation

> My challenge for you—you know there's always an actionable step!—is to have a conversation with somebody new.
>
> Maybe it's visiting a local business that you think aligns with your work. Maybe it's going to that

conference or arranging that coffee date with another business owner.

It's all about taking that first step to make a new connection that scares and excites you. This is the first step in getting other people to talk about what you do. That's how word-of-mouth works.

"

Collaboration over competition is where community grows.

Chapter 3
Brand You

Bhule: Marketing is just a logo and colours

Fuel: My business has a life of its own and marketing permeates every facet, interaction and touchpoint

Let's explore what your brand actually means, what value your brand brings, and what value you bring. This is really a great time to deep dive and get a little more vulnerable and visible in order to make sure that your messaging is on brand.

What does the word 'brand' actually mean? Well, it's not as simple as a logo and a font in a couple of colours—it really is the essence, the vibe, the feeling people get when they interact with your brand or company. Every single touchpoint needs to convey that feeling, from the first phone call or email exchange, all the way through to the customer's last experience with your brand before they move on.

The journey your customers take and their interactions with your brand need to get across that vibe and that essence.

Start to brainstorm all the different touchpoints—online and offline—that you might need to explore, using three words that encompass your brand's values.

When I started using this method, it changed the way I did my scheduling and my social media. It changed the way I connected with my clients in my bricks-and-mortar business and what my office looked like. It also changed the way that I would interact in public if I happened to see a client down at the local markets. It really informed the way that every single touchpoint occurred within my business.

Challenge
What do they see?

It's time to find out what other people see as your value—this can form the basis of your core brand values. It's easy to see our value as being our one-on-one consults, our products or a particular service, but often others see it differently. This is why you shouldn't only rely on your opinion of your core value.

You don't need to invest in a complex customer feedback campaign. You can start right now! Head over to your social media profile (personal or business) and simply ask, 'What do you see as my value?'

You will be amazed at the results. And there may be stories that come up too, especially if people's opinions take you by surprise and they value something you offer beyond the service you provide.

This is where you need to put your ego to one side and realise that listening to feedback is an exciting part of the branding process. You get to hear why people love you and now you can expand and grow that area of your offering (if you want to!).

This is the space to play with and lean into your first step in visibility and vulnerability.

Scheduling and visibility

Rule: You have to be everywhere at once for everyone to see you, and you have to do it all yourself

Fuel: Persistent and consistent is the way, and you can automate that

All of this connection, in all of the places on the internet and in person, can sometimes feel a little bit overwhelming, especially when we've got a lengthy to-do list already. It's hard to create time to work on our business *and* add one more thing—branding—to that to-do list. This is where scheduling comes in!

When I was growing my brand, I used to sit for an hour every Sunday and schedule the coming week's contents. Depending on the week, this would include my newsletter musings, what I was going to create on my social media channels, content for my blog post, and so on. Then it was as simple as scheduling that in.

There are so many content scheduling tools available for social media, especially for Facebook and Instagram. Scheduling content allows you to set and forget, so you can literally focus on your clients throughout the week and let your marketing tick along in the background.

Challenge
Five words for five days

Picking a content topic for each working day of the week takes the guesswork out of scheduling posts. These topics can be anything from your core work and business values, to sneak peeks behind the scenes.

In my clinic, we had a focus on women's health, inspiration, nature and science, and loved sharing what went on behind the scenes. Each of these topics became weekly posts sharing health tips for women, inspirational quotes, photos of our garden, the newest research, and small clips of our staff and the office.

Take some time to choose your five topics and post for the next five days.

Collaboration

Bhule: Don't share anything with anyone because they'll copy you, steal your clients and do better

Fuel: We are better together!

Collaboration over competition is something that I absolutely believe in no matter what I'm doing. I try to find a way that I can collaborate with another business and work with them for the common good of our clients.

Write down ten people you are inspired by, in business or in your field of work, and ten things that inspire your ideal client.

This is a way to find an overlap that can lead to collaboration. Many of my mentees over the years have connected and then collaborated on workshops, retreats, courses, and some amazing tools both online and offline as affiliates.

The rule of reciprocity is that when people receive something, they feel compelled to return the favour. One good turn deserves another. I see this as a universal law of mutually beneficial positive reinforcement.

If you love someone's work—if you resonate with what they do or how they help—it seems only right to acknowledge this in some way. Starting with this intention is the beginning of collaboration:

- What could you do right now to connect with the ten people who inspire you and start the flow of reciprocity? Could you reach out in an email, follow them on social media, support and share their work, direct message them, or even meet them in real life?
- Can you help somebody else create a message or connection that will ultimately help your clients and theirs?

One of my beliefs that I cultivated through affirmations is: what you place your intention on comes back to you threefold. It might not come back in the same way; it may be something totally unexpected, be it through clients, word-of-mouth, or some other amazing thing down the track. But until you put it out there, you won't know what it's going to result in. Reach out and connect and see what happens.

Communication

Bhule: We have to sound professional, otherwise people will think we don't know enough

Fuel: We are all human

There are three main ways that businesses engage with people, and I've personally done all three of them: business to corporate, business to business, and (what most commonly happens) PERSON TO PERSON.

In my naturopathic business, I was really excited about being able to run workshops for people in corporate jobs and companies. The benefit of educating groups is that you can increase your capacity to help more people. Plus, corporate workshops can be easily run during people's lunchbreaks.

In a proposal that I sent to my corporate clients, I pitched the concept of my workshops, including how they could specifically help their company to achieve their main objectives. After the third or fourth proposal, I managed to win over a big organisation. One workshop turned into a long-running series, which meant I could help roomfuls of people and gain extra income for my business.

I've also explored a business-to-business model—smaller businesses interacting with other small businesses. Focusing on what objectives businesses want to achieve, I created proposals and found myself in numerous meetings with businesses discussing what they needed.

In time, I came to realise that this approach was really lacking the human element. Yes, a well-strategised business proposal emailed to a contact can get you over the starting line, but it's not going to build loyalty or a genuine connection.

What actually got me over the line with these organisations—and what gets you over the line with anyone, be it one person or a thousand—is the human-to-human element. It wasn't until I engaged with the person from that company *as a person*—until I talked to them about their health, their hormones and their energy—that I was able to connect with them and make the progress that was needed in the business.

It was the human-to-human element that changed and shifted things for me—and the biggest thing that happens in these human connections is the storytelling.

I told these people stories about shifting energy. I told them stories about bettering their health and wellbeing through supporting their sleep. I told them about the changes that I personally noticed from taking time out and taking care of myself.

It was because of these stories, ones that made me feel vulnerable, that they wanted to engage with me on an ongoing basis.

Confidence is key

Rule: No one will listen to me

Fuel: It's not what you know, it's how you say it

Confidence is contagious. If you feel like you're in safe hands with someone, you can instantly relax in their presence. On the flip side, if the person who has promised to help you doesn't seem to trust their own skill set, you're going to question whether they can help you at all.

This doesn't mean it's wrong to have nerves—of course you will, especially when you're starting out with your business. It is, however, important to still back yourself despite those wobbles.

Trust that you are the person this person needs. Trust that you have the knowledge and life experience to deliver the service or product that is going to make their life better.

There are strategies you can use to boost your confidence faster, before you've even booked your first client or got your first customer. Explore affirmations that feel right for you (*My voice is my value, I am exactly where I need to be*) and stick them to your mirror. Spend time around people who believe in you, whether it's friends or your family. Start an 'evidence folder' of feedback from people you've helped, whether it's a collection of emails, texts, or direct messages to your social media.

Confidence doesn't always come organically, but you can help yourself on your way.

Less can be more

Bhule: All the successful people share absolutely everything on the internet; that's how they become successful

Fuel: You can share the scars not the scab to create connection and help others learn from your lessons

I remember the first thing I ever shared through my business account on Instagram. It took me days to pick a picture and find the exact words I thought would introduce my business in the right way. I agonised over it and whether it would have the right impact. I felt like it wasn't 'gritty' enough, when everyone else was posting such intimate content. I wanted to promote my business, but I also knew I needed boundaries; should I show images of my kids? Should I share my personal story? Should I share the stories of my clients?

It took me a lot of experience (and some uncomfortable overshares) to realise that you can say a lot and reach a big customer base without oversharing or overselling yourself.

I liken it to when I first fell over in front of my youngest child. As soon as I stood up, blood seeping out of the grit-speckled wound, it didn't matter what I said in that moment; my youngest wouldn't listen because there was just too much on show and it took away from the lesson. A week or so later, when the scab became a scar, it was much easier to let my youngest know that I should have been paying more attention down those stairs and what I could do next time to avoid it.

This section is all about sharing your story with grace and ease, without telling the world all about your bikini wax. So, we are going to tackle it in three segments:

The elevator pitch

You might have heard about the importance of the elevator pitch from way back in the day, but it really is the core of your message and helps you to explain exactly what it is you do when you meet someone for the first time.

Your story bank

Sometimes we get really caught up in telling a client all the facts, figures and things we do with health that we forget they're actually coming to ask something human to human, not human to expert.

Your story arc

How can you use your unique story to inspire your customers or clients and help people understand your services?

Your elevator pitch

For those who haven't been to networking events, there's a well-known concept called the elevator pitch, where you only get a certain number of seconds to share your story when (hypothetically) occupying an elevator with someone.

This is a brief moment to share how you can be of service to somebody and how that might also help your business. Sometimes it can feel weird and very salesy. The whole idea of the elevator pitch originated from the question: if you were to get in an elevator with someone, what could you sell to them in the moments before they reach their floor? And, I'd also add to that, how could you genuinely help them?

The script is as simple as:

> I help X people go from Y to Z through A services
> and B products, even if C presents a challenge.

Start to consider your ideal client and the journey you take them on. The first section is all about who you help, so start with 'I help'. This could be women, men, workers in a particular field, or certain communities.

You may help women as I did—maybe burnt-out entrepreneurial women.

If your niche includes more than one demographic, you could say something like, 'I help burnt-out women and their families.' But for the purpose of this exercise, it's best to stick with your ideal client.

The next thing to consider is the journey you take people on— this helps others understand the types of people you see right at the beginning and how you help them move through their journey and reach their goals.

'I take entrepreneurial women from burnt out to
fired up.'

What first steps do you take with clients? If their situation is
currently worst-case scenario, then how are you helping them
realise this when they first come to you? How are they presenting
to you, the first time you meet? And then, what is the best-case
scenario for what their life and health will look like at the end of
their journey, when they've finished with you?

Now we consider what type of offerings you implement to
help them move through that journey.

'I help entrepreneurial women go from burnt out to
fired up through workshops, webinars, retreats, and
one-on-one consults.'

Notice that you took the opportunity to introduce the idea that
you don't just do one-on-one consults; there are other ways
people can interact with you.

Lastly, you'll want to overcome the objections that some people
might have to working with you. Often, the biggest objections
have to do with time, ease or money. So, when it comes to the
final part of your elevator pitch, you might want to consider these
three areas, or any other big objections of your ideal client.

Take some time to brainstorm what the objections might be
for your ideal client, how you can take them on a journey, and
how you actually help them to move forward.

Your story bank

We are going to explore one of the ways we as humans have always connected—through storytelling. Humanity has used stories to connect since ancient history, when we all sat around campfires sharing lessons, experiences, traditions, knowledge, and all the beliefs and emotions that go along with these.

Have you ever really sat down and thought about your own story? As business owners, we spend so much time listening to others share their story or journey, but we need to remember that sharing our stories is also part of connecting.

Challenge
How you got here

Grab a pen and paper and start to brainstorm the experiences in your life that have moved you from a place of hardship to a place of overcoming.

This is a vital part of your story because your client is likely to be going through the exact same things you've been through. They may be experiencing hardship when it comes to their health, wealth, freedom and what they want to change, and they also want to overcome it. Giving yourself as an example by sharing your story is going to inspire them and create a motivation for change that you probably couldn't get by just giving them facts and figures.

I want you to do a little bit of detective work; drop into your past experiences and find those inspirational moments where you felt absolutely the most alive you ever have because you really did a lot of work to get there. It doesn't have to be about health in particular; it's just about identifying that feeling and the motivation for change you experienced so that you can easily get this across in your storytelling.

Now, there's a little trick for this—it's about identifying the high, the low and the high in your story.

What this means is that you first need to start with the high—an experience you had where you initially felt great.

Then the story moves into your moment of hardship—the low. When you're talking about the low, you need to really make sure that all the details are in there together so it's clear for your audience what emotions came up for you and how much of a challenge it was for you.

And then we end on the high—how you overcome your hardship and grow stronger than you were before.

In each of the stories and moments that you delved deep into your story bank to dig up, I want you to consider the high, the low and the high.

Your story arc

One of the most amazing moments I ever experienced was opening the doors to my clinic. I was so excited about opening my doors to all the people that I could help. I had so much knowledge and so many certificates and degrees on the wall. And I had also just bought my most prized possession: a microscope.

I opened the doors ... and nobody came for the first week. I thought to myself, *That's okay, I'll continue to do my work.* Nobody came the second week either, or the third week. By the fourth week of not seeing anybody, I felt really disillusioned. I'd managed to get all of these certificates on the wall, but I felt like a failure. I felt like an impostor, like I was never ever going to be able to turn this around.

Finally, I got online to do some research. But instead of researching health conditions that I'd already been researching for years, I started to research what it takes to create a successful business, both online and offline. Slowly but surely, I learned more and more about that side of my practice—and the clients started coming in. I kept putting into practice all the things I'd learned through my research, and eventually my business got so big in that first little clinic space that I needed to grow and expand. In the end, I created a multimodality practice that housed nine other practitioners as well as a dedicated workshop room—I even started running retreats and authoring books.

See what I did there? We started at the high, slowly descended into the detail of the challenge and the low, then came back up with the second high—coming out the other side stronger and more successful because of the challenge of the low. This structure is used by public speakers across the globe and it can help make your story more inspiring and engaging.

Another example of the high-low-high for me was when I was in burnout. I was seeing 1,400 clients a year and most of them were burnt-out mums. I made a name for myself as the practitioner that moved my clients from low energy and high stress to high energy and low stress—all in a relatively short period of time.

I absolutely loved what I did but I had started to notice I was eating less and felt more tired in the afternoons. Then I was accepted into a course in Bali. Two days before I was due to fly out, the course was cancelled and I was left with making the decision to go anyway or stay. After chatting with Murray, my husband, I decided to go anyway. I went over there thinking I would have so much time and space to keep working, but when I got there something hit me—I felt exhausted and fatigued, and my immune system dropped. I had Bali belly, I had pneumonia, I was in bed for three days, and I was all alone.

I didn't realise how exhausted I really was until I took time out to stop. And I realised in those moments that it was exactly the same situation I'd been helping my clients with for all that time.

After surrendering, I was able to recover, and for the next three weeks I began to write my book *Freedom from Fatigue*. I nourished myself with amazing food and I took opportunities for self-care through massage, connecting with nature, and connecting with my creative side.

When I came home, I was able to help others in a totally different way. I felt completely different and I knew that my time alone in Bali was meant to happen for this reason.

Can you see the high-low-high structure again in this example? You can use this structure in any mode of communication: events, retreats, webinars, workshops, blog posts, newsletters and social media posts. They all lend themselves to a high-low-high story.

Imagine you are doing a talk on hormones to an audience of women who are mostly aged 35 and up. You could talk about what keeps them up at 2:00 am—maybe they are waking with hot flushes. You tell them that by the end of the talk, they will have three strategies for combatting those hot flushes. You could throw in a story example—maybe a client case study that follows the high-low-high structure. These women are hooked and inspired.

You finish it up with an offer for them to book in and sign up to your newsletter.

Challenge
Your high-low-high stories

Your homework is to build a bank of ten high-low-high stories, either based around your health and wellbeing; a time you were able to overcome a challenge; or how you created a positive shift for any of your clients. And challenge yourself to tell one of these stories today, either through a blog post, social media post, newsletter or email.

Consider:

- What were three of the most challenging times of your life?
- What do you consider your greatest achievements?
- What is a moment you'll ever forget?

Sharing your whole self

For a long time, I was very careful (too careful) about the sides of myself I shared in my business, especially when it came to my spiritual beliefs. Not sharing my 'woo-woo' had me chopping off parts of myself to please others (stakeholders, clients, supplier companies) and therefore sacrificing speaking opportunities, educational pursuits, and target markets. Meanwhile, hiding my sexuality, not only from my community but also from my husband, stunted my voice and my purpose.

I hid what I used to call my woo-woo only until recently. Things under this banner include intuition, tarot cards, guidance cards, crystals, astrology and divination tools. I guess you could say my first business was reading tarot for travellers on the Eurail system to fund my adventures through Europe.

When working with clients I often have intuitive insights and visuals on how to best help and what questions to ask, that I couldn't get working empirically. As I moved into working with large corporate clients to put together my conferences, I was asked to focus on only the evidence-based parts of my presentations and veer away from some woo-woo topics in interviews; I came to believe that generally it wasn't to be talked about. The problem with that is it is like working with one hand behind your back. I know a lot of people in business who hide parts of themselves and their past that could bring real power and humanity to their work if they chose to share them.

Another part of my past that I was keen to keep quiet was my attraction to both men and women. I'm a cisgendered hetero-passing bisexual woman (monogamously married to a man) who's felt a mixture of shame and a sense of it being irrelevant. So, I just didn't talk about it—not to my husband and certainly not to my clients. Even when I was sitting in my clinic with clients whose anxiety stemmed from issues relating to sexuality.

I'll never forget when the Australian referendum for same-sex marriage came up and I discussed it with my hubby. We were both on the same vote—love is love—but it was through this discussion that I didn't just shrug off my past relationships. I put a label on it and really owned it for myself: bisexual.

Although I didn't go shouting this from the rooftops, something shifted in me and in how I used my voice. I noticed where I could bring attention to LGBTQIA+ causes through social media, charities or training. I shared and reposted educational content (including the use of inclusive language) written by diverse voices.

It took me three conferences to finally share the topic I was wanting to address, and to feel unrestricted in inviting speakers from all sorts of diverse backgrounds; I wanted to include a wide variety of personal stories and invite people to share their whole selves.

At this same conference I ran an intuitive circle and ceremony, as well as an empowering keynote. It was also at this conference that I had two attendees come up to me in tears and tell me it was the first time in their careers that they felt seen and welcomed in a professional setting for who they truly were.

It wasn't until I had embraced my whole self that I could share it with others.

You may not be ready to share your whole self in your business or personal life, but know there is great liberation in showing up unfiltered to your community. It also opens a door for you to use your experiences to help the people who are drawn to you—this is why they're here!

"

Courageous
conversation
creates
connection.

Chapter 4
Persistent and Consistent

Rule: Clients will find you when they need you

Fuel: Real relationships and support happen over time, when you're consistent and persistent

Keeping in touch via persistent and consistent messaging is so important. Did you know that it costs seventy per cent more time and money to engage a new client than it does to re-engage past clients? That means it takes seventy per cent more time and energy to create something new, have a conversation, or find a referral partner to get a new client. And it costs seventy per cent more money to get the marketing out into the world.

Where did you find your past clients, and how can you re-engage them by helping with other things? In business speak, we call it cross-pollinating when a client comes to see you for one thing, but you also teach them the other things you can help with.

The following are three easy ways to re-engage past clients:

1. A blog post, or video or audio upload
This blog post generally comprises a story, a teaching point and then an invitation; what is something that happened to you or a

client recently that you'd love to share—and what's the teaching point that you're wanting to get across? What was the thing that changed?

Then, create an actionable invitation at the end of your post to enable people to experience that same change by coming to see you.

2. A newsletter

An online newsletter is a great way of contacting a multitude of people in a very short period of time. So, if you currently have all of your past clients on a list or spreadsheet somewhere, or in your current booking system, now is the time to get them all on a central spreadsheet and save that as a CSV file. Take this file and upload it into your chosen mailing list program— these programs allow you to get that content out very, very quickly. As your business grows, this will allow your client list to grow with you.

At the time of writing, ConvertKit, Active Campaign, MailerLite and Mailchimp are email marketing platforms made for this purpose—these have more powerful features when it comes to email tracking, autoresponses and marketing funnels. Virtual assistants and technical assistants can help you to get started with email marketing using a platform that will best suit your business.

3. Social media

The third way to target past clients is by using social media. Facebook posts, especially when done consistently and persistently, are powerful at engaging and re-engaging clients. The posts that get the most engagement are usually personal stories.

Again, share using the high-low-high technique and then

follow it up with an invitation to connect with you further. This also goes for posting on other social media platforms like Instagram and LinkedIn.

Remember, you can always repurpose your content and post the same or similar versions of it across all of your different platforms. If you write a blog or newsletter, you could take teaching points out of those and post them on social media.

Challenge
The power of ONE THING

If nothing else, just creating one piece of sharable content per week could be a game changer for your marketing. Creating one thing that can then be repurposed saved me time, money, energy and sanity, and built a content library that I still refer back to to this day.

Through trial and error, I found that one of my best ways of sharing is doing live videos. I use the high-low-high story structure followed by a useful tip or lesson. I set a time each week to do one of these live training sessions and record it.

From there, my team and I:

- turn that one video into a blog post by transcribing it
- use that same transcription for a newsletter
- take out the five most useful tidbits to create social media posts for the week
- reshare the video on other platforms and social media channels

Find your best way of sharing. If you write well, do that. If you speak well, consider a podcast or audio recording. If you present well, then opt for video. Record. Repurpose. Share.

Take some time to think about 'just one thing' you could create and share. Don't overthink it; have fun with it and action it! You never know where that one thing could take you.

Shifting your sales mindset

As a new grad just out of university, my first job was in a health food store. My previous career was as a laboratory scientist in a hospital, so I had never had to 'sell' anything before. Being on the store floor as a sales assistant was an entirely new thing. I was so worried that the people coming in would have no money, that they would feel 'ripped off', that they wouldn't buy what I recommended and that I wouldn't do a good job.

Going into a conversation like that is like going on a first date when you are worried your breath smells. You do all sorts of weird things to get out of talking to the other human with you, and just focus on protecting yourself, so you come across weird and different to your usual self.

Once I changed my mindset around these conversations, everything changed. I showed up with confidence, people bought more and they even booked one-on-one consultations for more in-depth advice.

The shift I needed came in two ways:

1. Duty of care

The concept of duty of care is usually used in medical terms to describe doing your utmost, with the knowledge and experience you have, to take care of the person with you to the best of your abilities. If I am to truly be of service to the person with me, what would I prescribe and suggest, irrespective of cost? How would I service their needs, knowing to the best of my ability that it would help them? If it is not a product, what service would I recommend, and would they be better off seeing me for a more in-depth conversation so I don't miss anything in their complex situation?

2. Future pacing

The second shift is a well-known neurolinguistic programming technique called *future pacing*. It is having a conversation with the potential client not about what will happen if they take your suggestion on board, but if they do nothing. Pacing out a future in front of them and a vision for not changing can be a powerful motivator.

I have been asked so many times, 'Just *how* do you ask people to come and see you?'

'How do you ask them to get involved in your packages?'

'How do you get them to your webinars/workshops/seminars/e-course?'

So, I am going to take you on a little how-to-ask crash course.

The biggest thing to remember is that you're having a conversation; you're not 'selling' or asking people for money. It's actually the conversation, and letting go of the outcome of the conversation, that allows us to naturally move to the invitation. When you're inviting someone to come to your birthday party, they may say yes, they may say no, but you're not going to hold it against them if they say no because they've got something else on.

The same thing happens when it comes to your business—people have the opportunity to say yes or no, and attaching yourself to the outcome is only going to create a constricted energy between you.

This came naturally to me and it can come naturally to you too. Because all we're doing is asking some questions, creating an awareness of where the person is at on their journey, and giving them an opportunity to shift—then focusing on what they want and offering them a way to get that.

In the beginning, I didn't even realise I was naturally guiding my clients into the next consultation, the package, the plan for the next three months, or the next series of pathology tests. It wasn't about the details; it was about having the conversations that made them realise I could get them where they wanted to be.

So, this is how to begin the conversation:

> What is actually occurring for you at the moment?
> What does it look like in your body?
> How does it feel?

Get them to explain all of this in detail. It could be what they've gone through in their past or what they're currently experiencing. By asking them questions, you're creating their awareness. You're not telling them anything; you're simply asking questions.

Next, ask:

> Do you want to feel energised?
> Would you like to be sick a lot less often?
> How do you want life to look?

They may say something like, 'I want to have the energy to play with my kids.' Great! You'll need more clarity on that, so you might ask questions like:

> So what is holding you back, really?
> Have you prioritised yourself?
> What obstacles are stopping you from achieving these goals?

Get to their pain point. Get them to see what is holding them back.

They could be holding themselves back because they're not making their health a priority, they're choosing work over their health, they're choosing their kids over their health, or they're choosing time doing other things over their health. Obviously, nothing is going to happen if they don't change.

> 'What will happen if you don't change?'

> 'Well, everything will stay the same.'

> 'So, what is your plan then? If you'd like my help, I do have a Winter Wellness package that is available now—I know it'll be the best thing for you. Would you like me to book you in?'

What's different about this sales process is that the client is creating the awareness for themselves. They are taking themselves through the conversation and coming to the realisation that they don't have the answers and actually do need your help.

This process leads to the invitation to talk about your program, or their next consultation, or your webinar. It's up to them to decide whether your offering is their answer, or not. Even if they decide not to proceed, it has created awareness in them.

This process is sometimes called a discovery call.

Challenge
Who can you question?

Who could you have this conversation with over the next week? It doesn't have to be perfect, but at least you can start building those pathways to creating awareness, allowing them to ask for help and inviting them to work with you.

"

Stay curious.
Ask questions.
Create change.

Chapter 5
Mindset

Rule: It's all about the big vision and nothing else matters—this is entrepreneurship 101

Fuel: Any and all journeys begin with the first step

People who know me know I am an adventure girl. Freedom and holidays are my cornerstone and when I regularly have them, I have clearer mental health and my life is more abundant. But it wasn't always this way.

In the early years of my business, I believed my business couldn't survive without me. That if I wasn't there, there wouldn't be any money coming in.

A couple of years into my business and I was burnt out, juggling everything, seeing thousands of clients a year and having no breaks. I was starting to get resentful about clients wanting things from me and anxious in my home life. I knew I needed a holiday, but I really truly believed that if I wasn't at work, I would lose money.

I expressed this to a coach friend of mine and through the conversation, a new belief appeared: what if going on holidays is my best marketing tool?

I needed to start 'walking the walk' and showing my clients how to prioritise their mental and emotional health above anything. If I was working my way into burnout, how could I expect my clients to invest in their own life balance?

That thought became like a song you can't get out of your head and I soon booked a holiday to test it out.

This mindset shift changed the way I felt about going on holidays, which changed the way I behaved and the actions that I took. I shared my journey on social media and in my email newsletter and, sure enough, came back to an even busier office, with a record number of people having pre-booked while I was away.

Mastering your mindset

When it comes to business, your mindset is the most foundational tool that you have. Let's be honest, everything else you can google. Your mindset, however, is a personal lifelong experience—it can trip you up or it can be the tool that helps you move forward.

Mastering your mindset is the difference between hearing your mind say:

- *I'm not a good writer versus If I can write one word, I can write fifty thousand*
- *I'm not a great businessperson versus I have helped people before and made money from it, so I can do it again*
- *I'm not the greatest partner in the world versus It's exciting to find ways to show I care*
- *I pretty much fail at everything I do versus Failure is one step closer to finding a way that works*
- *Someone is going to find out how much I suck and that I*

am actually just making all of this up as I go along versus I'm so glad I'm giving this a go and learning so much through experience

Rather than having your mindset be the thing that derails your dreams and keeps you in bed hiding under the covers, it can become the fuel that keeps you going.

The pandemic changed so much for so many. Statistics show that it was a record year of unemployment and small businesses closing their doors, but in some sectors, it was actually their biggest year of growth yet. What is the difference between those that closed their doors and those that had their most successful year yet?

I would put forward that, in many cases, it was mindset—the ability to reframe, reassess, realign and move forward.

Mastering your mindset is a proactive strategy that doesn't come easily—but the hard work is so worth it.

Get ready to flex your mind as we:

- explore the concepts of integrity and commitment
- create a map for navigating your way through your flight plan
- go through the tools you need to create more time and focus

Where you're at

It's exciting to get to the end of a business goal, whether it's a project, the creation of a product or an income milestone. It's really hard, however, to know where you're going unless you know where you are at right now.

Those of us who are health practitioners will all have that

client who comes to us hoping for a miracle—who wants to get to an end point where they feel better. This client, however, is often completely unaware of where they are at when they start their journey.

In the health field, we check in with their diet and educate them about the different systems of their body that may be struggling, right here and right now. Their journey becomes clearer; they have a bit of a plan for getting where they want to go. But sometimes the client may not have all the facts about the true state of their health. They take a moment to realise the frequency of their headaches, the intensity of their pain, they realise their lack of water intake, minimal movement and even the toxicity in their environment. Sure, they may feel embarrassed, but it creates an awareness and a starting point for them to *choose* to change.

Often it's easier to see this in a health journey, but not so much when it comes to our own business. We often put our head in the sand about the facts of the matter. We become just like the client who lacks the awareness of where they're truly at—trying to ignore the data and just focus on the end result.

When I first looked at my numbers, I felt lost. I was second-guessing what was happening; I was making it up as I went along. When accountants, business coaches and advisors asked me questions, I wouldn't have any facts. I was worried and unsure. I was uncertain. I became really overwhelmed and I hid the facts, and by hiding them I became quite stuck.

It wasn't until I actually went and saw somebody and took the time to review everything that the shift happened. I sat down with a couple of bookkeepers and a couple of business mentors with my shoeboxes full of receipts. Now I could put the data on the table and see where things were lacking and where they were abundant.

Although the numbers weren't what I wanted them to be, I felt empowered. I felt secure and confident in the decisions I had to make and where I actually had to spend or save money.

This was the same with clients. My clients were becoming more profitable and more committed to their health goals; they were the ones who really made me feel like I was in the flow.

I reviewed the data around my marketing numbers—at the time, Facebook was doing better than my website, so I could make informed decisions around where to spend my marketing time.

I was moving forward with clarity, rather than just plucking things out of thin air.

Challenge
Get cosy with your numbers

This exercise will give you a snapshot of what's happening in your business right now, so that you can figure out what you want and how much time and energy it'll take to get there.

- Write it down on paper how many clients you have per week and how much potential cash per week is coming in. On a scale from 1 to 10, how well do you think you're going with it?
- What about your website—do you have one? Are you creating content? If so, how often? Write down on paper how many touchpoints people have to see you online.
- What is your social media reach like? Do you have accounts on multiple platforms, and are you using them?
- What systems do you have in place? What

business tools do you use? Are you going to upgrade? How can booking be easier for clients? What support do you have? Where are you doing things that aren't in your 'zone of genius'?

The juice on judgement

Rule: Judgement is bad and everyone is judging you

Fuel: Judgement happens to all of us—it is an innate, unconscious part of being human

Most of us are not aware of our judgements. This is because judgement can be part of automatic, unconscious programming that we picked up from the past—usually from earlier times in our lives, often from our parents or caretakers, or the reactions of others.

Experiences we live through—and the result of those experiences—often dictate how we react when similar things happen to us in the future. The judgement we receive from others at the time of the experience can be taken on as our own. And we react based on these past experiences in order to keep ourselves safe.

When I was seventeen, finishing off year 12 and having to choose what I was going to do with the rest of my life, I asked my dad for advice. Given I was excelling at English and art, I was excited about the prospect of doing a degree in arts. I was taking chemistry, biology and physics as well and did okay in those. On asking Dad, his off-the-cuff sarcastic remark was 'Do you know what skills you get from an arts degree? The ability to say "Would you like fries with that?"'

Although the experience was just my dad saying less than two dozen words, the way I reacted to that shaped my next decade. Fearing his judgement, I ran full force into a degree in Medical and Applied Biotechnology.

ABR: Attitude, behaviour, results

The *attitude* that we have around things (or the judgement or the label) influences the way we *behave,* which impacts ourselves or other people, creating certain *results.*

Attitude is how we are being, *behaviour* is what we are doing with that, *results* are what we have from that.

If we are constantly creating our future based on how we feel about the past, and behave as we have in the past, then we are going to see the same result over and over again. Before we know it, we're stuck in a cycle.

What happens when we want to purposefully change the future and achieve different results? We need to create an awareness of our attitudes and judgements.

Let's take shallow breathing, for instance. When we take a deep breath, we start to notice our behaviour—we start to notice that we actually need to breathe more deeply.

So, if we start to notice that we're feeling stressed and then notice that we have been shallow breathing, we can start breathing deeply to rectify this. But in order to change the behaviour, we need to create an awareness of when this happens, what it took to change it, and the results we got.

The same thing can happen with a judgement. Perhaps you believe a competitor or colleague is doing better than you (we've all been there!). Perhaps this makes you feel like you want to hide away and give up. Or maybe you feel 'less than' as a business owner. This will then impact how you act in your business—whether you put yourself out there or act small and miss opportunities.

When we catch ourselves in a moment of judging either ourselves or someone else, we need to explore those thoughts in order to see how we can change our attitude and behaviour to create a different result.

Challenge
ABR in action

Grab your journal and explore the following questions:

- Can you think of an area in your life where you can see the ABR model in action?
- What shifts do you think you can make when you focus on your attitude?
- What else influences this model (internal or external)?
- What do you think the ripple effects are when we focus on our attitudes?
- How could you apply this to a specific goal or challenge you have right now?

Befriending the green-eyed monster

In the early stages of my career, envy and the green-eyed monster had me hooked in a cycle of comparisonitis. I would see someone else succeeding in my industry and feel a prickle of *Why not me?* It made me see other practitioners as my competitors, when really we had so many opportunities to learn from each other and help each other grow.

I also have to admit, however, that envy had upsides. Seeing what was possible made me all the more motivated to do it bigger and better. It gave me motivation to change the status quo and take it all to a new level.

When I began attending professional conferences, I noticed that a lot of male practitioners were on stage talking about issues relating to women. Now, there's arguably nothing wrong with this if they are experts on the subject, but some of them didn't seem to have the basic experience or knowledge needed to contribute to the subject in any meaningful way (let alone demonstrate compassion for common female issues). Many of the conferences I attended seemed disorganised, outdated, boring and just plain uncomfortable.

Although I was envious that some of these companies could get so many members of our profession in one room for a conference, I could also see how it could be done differently.

I used the energy to see if it could shake up the status quo—and the whole conference scene. I decided that the old-school way of doing conferences might work for old-school ways of being, but it didn't work for me anymore. And, if it didn't work for me, there must have been at least ten other people it didn't work for either.

So I pulled it apart!

I asked myself: instead of complaining about what I didn't like, what if I thought about what I *would* want?

I started to write a list of what I would like. How could I flip everything that I didn't like about a conference for our profession into something that I would love to go to—that I wouldn't nag about. That I wouldn't whinge about. That I would get excited about.

The old-school way
- Academia
- Selecting speakers who can spruik the latest products
- Glitzy closed rooms
- No natural light
- Sandwiches for lunch

The new way
- Inspiration, personal development and business development, as well as academia
- Jumping in ball pits
- Healthy, radiant food
- Yoga and movement and self-care (as a way of being throughout a conference rather than an add-on)

I changed it up from first being envious and getting frustrated about the line-up, to picking new up-and-comers and giving them a stage to start speaking their truth. And, instead of an us-versus-them model, I supported collaboration over competition.

Since then, I have run multiple conferences in person and digitally, with attendees joining from six countries and every state of Australia. My team and I have also welcomed thousands of attendees to our events and retreats, and had amazing feedback.

I've also noticed the distinct change in other professional conferences to include health and wellbeing as standard, digital tools for accessibility, and healthier food and light.

I know this wouldn't have been possible if the green-eyed monster had not visited me and shown me my desire to change the experience of watching someone on stage.

Whenever you notice envy and frustration towards something, whether it's in your business or wider profession, know you have the power to change it. There's a reason it has lit up for you, so pay attention and use that energy not for evil, but for good; as much as you may want to tear it down, that same energy can be used to build it back up in a more helpful way. And it's yours, there for the taking.

You can create the new status quo.

When imposter syndrome struck

In June 2015, I decided to sell my practice—the practice I had built up from nothing. At the time, we had a huge multi-six-figure turnover; nine different practitioners serving seven thousand people in our amazing community; an incredible referral system and word-of-mouth network; a beautiful light-filled space; and regular workshops. Time disappeared when I was with my clients—forty-five of them a week.

It was a success, from a business perspective, without a doubt.

But I was also burning out quickly. And I knew it was a great time to sell.

On the inside, I felt like I was chasing my tail; I was constantly trying to innovate new projects, but wasn't finishing them. I also wanted to get some work-life balance back.

It felt like I had created a machine, and now the machine was controlling me.

One of the practitioners I worked with was excellent at what she did and was as committed to community health as I was. She could see a vision for the practice that I couldn't moving forward. We were both excited for her to take the reins—but that came with a lot of logistics!

There're the business meetings, the broker meetings, the accountants and the bookkeepers. There's the legal side: the 81-page handover document as an ongoing concern. All this at the same time as running a multimodal practice so that it keeps on being prosperous.

One afternoon I realised, while I was paying all the bills, that my car's registration ran out that day. In the toing and froing of getting the business ready for sale, I had forgotten to pay my registration.

I quickly got the mechanic around to do what he needed to give me a pink slip and proceeded to try to pay for the registration online. For some reason my credit card didn't work. I thought, *Oh, I'll just pay it in the morning.*

Of course, on the way home the following day, I got pulled over by a highway patrol vehicle.

'Do you know why I've pulled you over today?' the officer asked.

'Yes,' I replied. 'Actually, I've tried paying my registration …'

'You knowingly left the house this morning, in an unregistered vehicle, with your children in the car?'

She handed me a $697 fine and told me I needed to go to the nearest service centre and pay the registration. This meant I would have to get somebody else to take my kids to school, as I couldn't drive until it was organised, so I had to ring my mother-in-law to help. Suddenly, I couldn't stop my tears from flowing.

On top of all of the money that was changing hands in the process of handing over a business, and all the numbers that I had to crunch into a spreadsheet, $697 was the straw that broke the camel's back. For me, $697 represented a failure.

I was selling a successful business, but I felt like an imposter. For giving it up. For having dreams outside the business that I had thought would be my everything.

These words meant to me that I'd not only failed in my business, but I'd also failed as a parent. And if I'd failed as a parent, then I must have failed as a practitioner. And if I was failing as a practitioner, then, then, then, then ...

All this wonderful braiding continued, and so did the tears.

As the tears fell I thought, *If I were my own client, what would I say to me right now? If I were my client, I'd tell me to ring a friend.*

So, I tried to ring my husband, but he wasn't available. I tried to ring my mum, who's always available ... but she didn't pick up this time. I tried to call an ex-coach of mine and, although she didn't pick up, she sent me a message:

Are you okay?

It was these three little words that got me ... because I wasn't okay. But I wasn't the person that's not okay. If I wasn't okay, what did that say about me?

Then, another thought crossed my mind: *What would happen if I was okay about not being okay?*

As I stepped out of the service centre, onto the footpath, I hung my head and took a moment to mull over this thought. Suddenly, a quote from Dr Seuss reminded me: I have feet in my shoes and I can go wherever I choose. It was a very timely reminder of my privilege and gratitude.

I thought, *Even if I'm handing my business over to somebody else, I have the capacity to build this—and more—again. I have those skills and talents. I have three incredible kids who trust me to take them to school. And trust me to look after them. Who love me, as I love them.*

All of those little things that I had been scared about, that I was sure I was failing at, were actually some of the biggest lessons I've ever learned.

Instantly, about fifty per cent of my sobbing stopped. And I thought, *Wow, that's amazing. That's the real power of mindset and the stories that we choose to tell ourselves, or not.*

Of course, mindset isn't a magic pill you can swallow. You have to work at it. Since then, I've learned to emotionally nurture myself, especially during busy times in my business.

For me, nurturing a positive mindset now looks like:

- Surrounding myself with supportive people going through a similar journey
- Asking for help before I need it
- Taking time out for nature, baths and movement to reset my feel-good hormones
- Working from inspiring places and not just the same place all the time
- Setting the tone for the day by journalling and pulling guidance cards
- Seeing a coach or practitioner who will remind me to reframe my thoughts and nourish myself properly

Challenge
Your positivity prompts

Of course, you're welcome to follow my feel-good rituals, but it's also so empowering to invent your own. Take a few minutes to think about what actions, hobbies or rituals make you shine. Write down a list of them and stick it on your fridge so that it's impossible to forget or ignore them; then a positivity prompt will be always at your fingertips.

Integrity

Rule: Fake it till you make it

Fuel: There is no replacement for authenticity and integrity when it comes to making it: be it, until you see it

Imagine you're in the kitchen cooking a meal and you leave a little mess that you don't clean up. Then the next mealtime comes around and you start cooking again, which creates a bit more mess on top of the mess that you already had. If you leave it, another mealtime will come around and eventually you will have such a big mess that it's hard to clean up. This can be like the concept of integrity.

Integrity is a core concept that you need to understand and implement if you are going to be a successful entrepreneur and lead an unrestricted life.

Integrity *(noun)*
1. the quality of being honest and having strong moral principles.
2. the state of being whole and undivided.

Now, when we hear the word integrity, we often think about following through with the things that we say we'll do. That's one of two ways to view it; integrity is also the notion of speaking your truth and using your words as a tool.

When words come out, they have a power and an energy about them. When we make a promise or an agreement with somebody, then we try to follow through and give it one hundred per cent. This also rings true for the words and promises we tell ourselves, but too often we don't commit to our own agreements.

We can also think of integrity like the wheel of a bike—the whole wheel is held up by numerous spokes. When there's one little niggle in a single spoke, it's only a matter of time before there are bigger problems. If we ignore this little niggle, eventually the spoke becomes compromised and the entire wheel ends up losing integrity.

The same thing can happen in your business when you tell yourself those little lies about what you have or haven't done, or hide the to-do lists that you know you need to act on to move your business forward. These are the things that may start out as a niggle, but if ignored can cause a huge lack of integrity. We call them open loops.

We need to close the loop on these niggles, these gaps, these to-do lists. An open loop could be an unopened email, or a chat thread or text message that you haven't responded to. It could be an invoice you haven't completed or something that you need to follow through with for your clients.

The problem with keeping these loops open is that you end up expending energy worrying about the niggles instead of addressing them and moving on. This energy could be channelled into creating amazing things in your business.

We need to focus on doing what we say we will do, within the timeframe we say we'll do it. Even when promising to show up for your kids, or family members. It's those little excuses that we need to be aware of: excuses like 'I can't, it's raining,' or the white lies you tell when you are trying to get out of something you initially committed to.

Sometimes we have genuinely not been able to complete something by a certain time, but part of maintaining integrity is recommitting to an action to get it done—not just in your head, but to the person you made the commitment with. Own it, clear it up, recommit.

There is so much freedom when we stop making justifications and getting consumed in our story. Excuses often mean you're out of integrity.

Remember, it's not just maintaining integrity with others (many of us like to think we keep our word), but it is also all the times that we have the opportunity to rebuild integrity within ourselves and close our own loops.

Challenge
Closing loops to get back into integrity

Grab a piece of paper and brainstorm all the places and spaces where you are currently out of alignment with your integrity and could take action to close those open loops.

Open loops take up bandwidth in our thoughts. You will often find them as recurring 'should' thoughts, things like *I should get back to that email, I should be doing the taxes, I should respond to that text message, I should finish off that client report, I should book that doctor's appointment.*

These open loops may also be a big project that's been at the bottom of your to-do list for a longer time than expected. But when you begin to take action towards completing it, it actually takes significantly less time than you expected, and you wonder why you hadn't done it earlier.

Lastly, closing loops takes courageous conversations—have the courage to admit that things may take longer than you expected, or that you may have made other things a priority, or that things have changed. These difficult yet seemingly simple conversations can get us back into integrity.

Going all-in!

Your success lies in going all-in.

My son plays basketball, and some days he doesn't go all-in: he doesn't play full-out. Sometimes he plays at twenty per cent.

But the days he plays full-out, and puts in one hundred per cent effort, he gets one hundred per cent results. If he's not shooting for a point, he's high fiving, everybody is excited—himself included—and he knows he hasn't left anything behind.

I want that for you as well. Otherwise, we end up sitting in the bleachers, watching everybody else play full-out. I want you to be on the court, playing as hard as you can; because what you get out of it at the end is so much bigger, so much more rewarding, than just sitting on the sidelines.

In Brené Brown's book *Daring Greatly,* she quotes Roosevelt:

> It is not the critic who counts; not the man who points out how the strong man stumbles, or where the doer of deeds could have done them better. The credit belongs to the man who is actually in the arena, whose face is marred by dust and sweat and blood; who strives valiantly; who errs, who comes short again and again, because there is no effort without error and shortcoming; but who does actually strive to do the deeds; who knows great enthusiasms, the great devotions; who spends himself in a worthy cause; who at the best knows in the end the triumph

of high achievement, and who at the worst, if he fails, at least fails while daring greatly, so that his place shall never be with those cold and timid souls who neither know victory nor defeat.

What does playing full-out look like for you?

Chapter 6
Value, Leverage

Bruce: Everyone is an individual and we need to treat everyone differently

Fuel: There are commonalities to everyone, and the unique way you take people on a journey is leverageable

To create wealth and sustainable growth, we need to consider how we can create value, and then leverage it. The value we can create is around ideas, knowledge and innovation. It's also around the area of service and how you supply that service.

As entrepreneurs, we are full of value; we have brains that hold so much knowledge and so many ideas that we are able to share. We are so extraordinary, yet too often we are a bit blind to that fact. It can be a bit of a treasure hunt to see the value that you currently have.

You need to look at value as how *valuable* you are to others, and then you can look at how to *leverage* that.

The first aspect of leverage is using relationships to grow your value—especially with those who have a big group of people around them, or perhaps a client base that is complementary to yours. Your network increases your net worth.

The second aspect of leverage involves details and systems.

When it comes to your value, we are looking at all of the things that you currently value, *and* what you currently sell that's valuable. For instance, a consultation is a valuable asset. We then have the ability to leverage value with follow-up consultation and, more often than not, a supporting product.

These examples are generally found in the offline world, but they can also be leveraged online.

There is value in your facts sheets, an e-course, a blog post. All of those things you have half written or recorded? There's value in them too.

Take stock of exactly what those areas are—the areas in which you know you can create value.

The offline component of leverage is around referrals and your network. As I've mentioned, we want to create a relationship or conversation with potential referrers who all have similar groups of people connected to them.

The second aspect of leveraging involves using digital systems. In the online world, using social media is a fantastic, easy, cheap way of getting your message out and putting forward invitations to have conversations. Other great systems include autoresponders, email newsletter sign-ups, marketing tools and customer relationship management software.

If your value lies in packaging up visits to come and see you, there needs to be a mechanism by which new clients can hear about this. A quick way to leverage this value is to send out an email, or post about it on your social media page.

So, what are the systems that you need in order to leverage the value that you have? And how are you going to get your message out to the right people so that they come to you, see your value and invest in you?

Signature system (your formula)

Your signature system is your unique formula. The way we do one thing is the way we do everything, whether it comes to our business or our life goals. The comforting and powerful truth is, if we can come up with a signature system—and lean into it— we're far more likely to achieve our ambitions.

You'll recognise the four steps in my own system if you've read my book, *Freedom from Fatigue*. The four steps are:

1. **Remember who you are.** For me, forgetting this step is how I got myself into a state of adrenal fatigue. It's about how I created opportunities for my clients to heal from adrenal fatigue. I also came to realise that remembering who I was, was the driving force behind why I was making the decisions I was making in my life. I would remember to realign with my core purpose, my core mission and my core values.
2. **Remove obstacles.** The next step is about removing negativity and anything that is standing in your way. I worked to remove hidden obstacles to health and wellbeing.
3. **Look at what you're working with and refine it.** What does the refinement step look like? It looks like refining how you look after yourself and refining what is actually beneficial for you. It is going from good to great.
4. **Recharge.** It's important to remember that all of us need to retreat and recharge ourselves from time to time.

What steps are you taking to create your signature system? Step 1, 2, 3, 4, or something else? It could be fewer steps, or more. Choosing what steps to take can be made easier by looking at what steps you take elsewhere in your life.

Remember, the way you do one thing is the way you do everything.

The Get Shit Done Post-it Note Method

Bhule: Creating a course is confusing and
hard—don't bother

Fuel: There are simple steps to get shit done

Welcome to Get Shit Done Post-it Note Method. This is a process to help you take your signature system and put it into a logical, teachable sequence. You can use this method to reduce the overwhelm that often comes with the idea of putting a course or program together. It allows you to get it all out of your head like a massive brain dump—and then you can start to filter through the content.

There are three different sections in this method, so it's ideal to have Post-it Notes of three different colours to choose from. (Having a colour system isn't necessary, but it definitely makes the process a lot easier.)

- **Yellow Post-it Notes** are your major topics and modules; your broad areas of knowledge and specialist skill sets (e.g. detox).

- **Blue Post-it Notes** are teaching points—more specific areas of advice and targeted guidance (e.g. probiotics).

- **Green Post-it Notes** are for resources and/or things you need to create. This could cover things like PDF handouts, checklists, audio files, videos, cooking demos, interviews—whatever resources are needed to support the blue teaching topics, and make it easier for the user to grasp the concepts and apply them to their life.

- **Now take a bird's-eye view of your Post-it Notes.** Does achieving all this look doable or like too much hard work with not enough reward? That is the beauty of this method—it allows us to see an overall snapshot of a whole plan and what will actually be needed in order for us to create it. If it looks like it's too much, start culling some ideas or maybe move them aside to be used later in another course or program.

- **Putting it into action.** Once you have a plan laid out that you're happy with, it's time to look at who you'll need on your team and what technology and methods you will need to employ to make it all happen. Do you need a virtual assistant? A video editor? What apps will you need to sign up to in order to create your audio files or host content like your videos? Where will you be able to 'batch' tasks and get similar things done in one day?

- Another way to look at this is to consider what teaching points or resources you could potentially repurpose into other content for your social media, newsletters, and so on. There will be so many nuggets of gold that you can easily run as themes through your content creation or even as mini challenges.

Let's get real about passive income

Bhule: Passive income is so easy and everyone should do it: set and forget

Fuel: Structure enables flexibility

Passive income is the catchcry of the online marketing world, which often touts 'make money while you sleep' with zero effort involved. While one common side effect of passive income systems is actually making sales at any time of the day, there is considerable effort involved to systemise and produce products or services so they're available, and to maintain it.

The real benefit is moving from exchanging time for income, to creating services or products that are pre-recorded and/or available, without you being present or your time being spent.

If you are at the very beginning of your business, you will need to be focused on bringing in the money and creating cash flow rather than setting up passive income streams. Creating passive income takes a lot of time and work, and takes time away from earning your income while you are establishing yourself.

Once you are up and running, however, there is no reason why you shouldn't consider creating some type of passive income.

Packages and plans

Bhule: One-on-one consulting is the best and only way to help

Fuel: Partnering with clients on a journey benefits the client, the service provider and the business

Packages are a way that we can group a series of consults together for our clients to provide them with long-term care and help them achieve their goals. This is a lot like a gym membership—when you sign up, you don't just sign up for one visit then you're done.

The gym has got it right in that, once you pay for it, you are far more likely to keep showing up: there's literally a commitment of time, energy and money that motivates you to get the result that you are looking for.

The same thing will happen with your clients—a package creates an opportunity for the client to commit to their long-term goals.

The other benefit of providing a package is that it will give you a quick cash injection into your business, because people pay upfront; if you create a package with a certain amount of consults designed to take the client through their journey, it will generally provide an injection of cash that you wouldn't necessarily get by them paying consult by consult.

Equally, if they choose a payment plan, you'll have a steady and consistent level of funds hitting your business over a number of weeks or months. It can also be enticing for clients to not have to pay a large amount of money upfront. You can use this consistent cash flow to pay for supplies, upgrades and even staff.

In order to create a package or a plan, there are some the things that you need to consider:

1. **You need to know your client.** You need to know who your ideal client or target market is and what their journey might look like. Knowing your client is very important because taking a cookie-cutter approach to creating a package might not be the right thing for your particular group of clients, in your particular area of the globe, for the things that you particularly like to help with. Your client might not be interested in the detox package, but their eyes might light up when they see the energy boost package. They might not be interested in a profits package, but they might really want a package that will help with buying their dream house.
2. **You need to know the journey.** The quickest way to ensure that somebody will be willing to come along for the ride is knowing exactly what ride it is they need to take.

TAMMY GUEST

So, in my world, when I was treating adrenal fatigue clients, I knew that at the beginning of the journey they would likely be resonating with terms such as 'exhausted', 'tired', 'unfocused', 'having trouble concentrating', 'really want to nap in the afternoon' or 'forgetful'—and then four weeks in I knew they would feel so amazing that they'd want to go climb a mountain or run a marathon.

I knew exactly when the perfect check-in times would be for their program, what our conversations would focus on, and what kinds of supplemental support they'd need.

After eight weeks they would feel generally rebalanced and be sleeping better, feeling energised and feeling empowered, and able to put in place a maintenance plan for their adrenal health.

Knowing the journey that you want to take your clients on is really important. What is coming up for them—the good, the bad, and all the rest—and what you can do to support them in each of those moments? Is it the information that you can share? Is it a conversation that you can have? Is it supplements, or something else?

It's all about the details

The next thing you need to consider when it comes to packages is the details. Are you going to create a package that has products included, or not? Are your clients going to have the option to pay upfront, or will there be instalment options?

Payment is really important because your clients are not just paying for an initial and follow-up consultation—they're paying for the results they will get over the time that they're with you.

The payment for packages is going to be different—payments are going to be spread out over time and you will need to consider what you will do with them, as well as what works for your clients and their journey.

Once you have your payment structure sorted out, the next thing you will need to do is decide how you will ensure your clients are able to choose the right package for them. It can be helpful to create a discovery call or initial chat for clients so that you can see what package would be suitable or decide what else might be needed.

Automation is a breath of fresh air
Lastly, there is automation—this is the brilliance of having the internet and including online offerings in your packages. Automation is an easy way of keeping in touch with your clients without having to be there all the time.

So, instead of having a phone call on the fourth week, or your client coming in for a follow-up consultation when you know they are going to tell you that they are just about to undo all the good work they've been doing, you instead set up an automated email to go out during that week, saying something like, 'Okay, I know that you are probably considering undoing all your great work now because you feel amazing, but instead, check out this fact sheet about what is *actually* going on.'

Where you can, send an email that provides resources like a fact sheet, a shopping list, a swap sheet (a list of alternatives), mini training, or a checklist about what they might be feeling or going through. It all depends on where they are headed on their particular journey and the package they have chosen.

If you're creating that journey, how could you automate the package so that there is more value, but you're not actually placing any extra time, effort or energy into it (except for the set-up of course)?

I'm going to give you an example of a two-month change package:

- **The first impression:** Firstly, there will be an initial testing appointment to see where the client is at. This could go for an hour or more—it's up to you. This is where you get to know your client, their history and their desires, and do testing as required. You're building a relationship, and creating trust in that relationship.

- **Engagement and education:** On the first day, as they are starting their journey, an automated email will be sent out that is centred around 'the freak out'. The freak out is in response to the change that's about to happen; things they were doing before now have to stop and be replaced with new routines and tools. Your automated email will give them advice and encouragement around what they're going to need to change, some type of downloadable that rocks their world so much they want to stick it on their pin board, and an idea of what to expect for day one. By doing this, you are facilitating engagement and education without actually having to be there.

- **Reassurance:** A week or two in—at the beginning of the shift—your client may have some resistance to the changes, and may be having a hard time. This is where you'll want to get in touch, via an automated email, to let them know that this is totally normal and that it will pass, and invite them to ask any questions.

- **The check-in:** Midway through, they will likely start to feel good. This is a good time to automate another email, perhaps sharing something new—a lesson or an insight— that will help them move from A to B. This would also be a good time to discuss opportunities on social media platforms, in training programs or online videos to connect, upsell other services or products that could help, and set the ideas or intentions about what they might want to achieve by the end.

- **The next level:** Beyond halfway, your client is going to be feeling fabulous and telling other people about how they are doing, what changes they've made, and the big changes they've noticed in themselves. This is the time to build on that momentum and how excited they are about the improvements they've noticed so far. There is opportunity here to bring in the different levels of information that might have been overwhelming in that first week. Repetition and reminders of how far they have come are invaluable here.

- **The long-term plan:** The final training exercise or session is an opportunity for you to reconnect with your client, remind them of their goals and intentions, invite them to come and see you again for further support, and make sure that they have clarity around their options post-program. Some of your clients may choose to go into a longer-term program or membership where you can give them ongoing sessions in a group setting.

Within all of this automated content, you can include checklists, recipes, fact sheets, reflective journaling prompts, ebooks, swipe files, questionnaires, video training and quizzes, and even an audio recording or meditation.

Now, this is a generalised example, but it could be adjusted and translated for all kinds of industries as a framework for building rapport, creating a relationship of trust, gaining momentum and putting a long-term plan in place. It's about offering value and then leveraging it, so your relationship can continue to offer even more value.

The million-dollar question—pricing!

A few years into my business, I moved to a new premises. After moving from serviced offices to a shopfront four times the size and seeing hundreds of clients, I knew it was time to put my prices up. Despite all my intuition (and my data) saying it was the right time, the angst I felt and the worry I had went on for weeks. My inner critic swirled in my head: *What would people say? What would they think of me? What if I lost all my clients? What if no one came due to the new prices?*

Despite this voice and my internal doubt, I increased my pricing anyway. I doubled my initial consultation fee for new clients. And, do you know what happened? Nothing, except that the clients who came in were more motivated than usual.

At the same time, I realised there were only so many people I could see in a day, and I was seeing them all. So, instead of selling single one-hour time slots, I decided to take my clients on a journey instead—a series of consultations, resources, training exercises and experiences all grouped together in a program.

Pricing for this seems even more complicated to begin with, but apart from the overheads, it really does come down to an energetic call of value exchange. As a practitioner, imagine the value of offering longer-term support with losing weight, resolving health conditions or falling pregnant.

It is not simply a matter of the cost of each part of the program it's the intangible things like a healing relationship, connection, communication, and the nuances of the way you do things.

When it came to pricing my program, I didn't really have another business to compare to, as I wanted my programs to provide a unique service. Eventually I thought about a price that would feel uncomfortably low, then a price that would be uncomfortably high … and finally came to a stretch number in the middle. It felt comfortable enough to ask for, but also stretched into my goals … and I knew could provide those results for my clients.

What's more, I decided to start talking about it immediately (in the interest of backing myself!). When I sat down with my first client the following week, I invited her to my program, knowing it could really help her. She didn't flinch and signed up immediately. I've loved running programs ever since.

When it comes to pricing up a package, you have to look at it from a bird's-eye view, including all the additional resources, email contact, bonus products and anything else you'll be bundling with it.

You are building a longer-term, supportive relationship—and that is valuable. You are giving your client valuable information at precisely the moment they need your support. So, the cost of the entire package, including the support provided by the automated emails, higher than the sum of its parts—and the results that clients are going to get are worth that.

Case study
a detox package

A great example of this is a detox package. In my clinic, this package might cost $800. This seems like a lot to some people, but let's break down the value.

What's it worth to have a kickstart?

What's it worth to lose 3–5 kilograms within two weeks (if that's one of your goals)? What's it worth to cleanse your bowel and your gut?

What's it worth to reset your hormones?

What's it worth to address your vitamin and mineral deficiencies and experience better sleep in two weeks?

What's it worth to decrease your fluid retention?

And what is it worth to know that the majority of the people who bought this package have had great results in the same two weeks?

For most people, $800 is less than what they'd spend on their cat, so to feel all of these health benefits in such a short period of time is extraordinary value for money. It's also extraordinarily beneficial to follow a detox in this way.

If you find that your clients are worried about the price, then allowing them to pay it off over time in a payment plan is going to make it easier for them to say yes: for example, they might pay it off in four easy payments of $200.

A successful sale of this detox package will involve:

- Minimal extra time and effort if you incorporate automation
- Understanding your client's journey and supporting them at each step through automation
- Offering supportive products and training that your client might need (if they want to include that in the price)
- Discussing the benefits that your

client will experience if they make the commitment.

Standing out and showcasing yourself

Rule: Service providers should do quiet work in the background

Fuel: I have an incredible message that needs to be seen and heard

Here are some really simple but powerful tips and tricks when it comes to creating training videos and webinars. Videos and webinars are brilliant tools for your business, and you don't need to be a natural actor to do them (I promise!).

The gear!
Camera first. This essentially captures all the visual aspects, so it has to be clean and clear. Make sure that the actual lens is clean by giving it a wipe with a soft cloth. Next, make sure the device is fully charged, and on aeroplane mode if it's a phone. If you're recording on a computer, ensure that the software is up to date so you don't encounter any glitches.

The set-up
Before you hit record, make sure that your camera isn't too close to you—like you're hijacking someone's personal space—or too far away. A good distance is an arm's length away from the camera. And give yourself about two metres between you and your background.

Speaking of your background, make sure it is clean and clear and that no items stand out—you want the attention drawn to you.

The gaze

Position the camera so that it's level and at eye line—you don't want any funny angles. In the video, your eyes should be about a third of the way down from the top of the screen. When you're recording, make sure you're looking at the camera itself and not at your computer or phone screen.

The lighting

The next big thing to think about is lighting. You want to make sure that the lighting on you is natural, soft and diffused. Make sure there are no shadows and that the light hits your face evenly.

The audio

You want people to be able to hear you well. The most basic option is to use your computer or phone's built-in microphone, or you could even use the mic on your earphones if you don't mind the cord. Just be aware that these mics can pick up background noises too—so if a garbage truck goes by outside, that may well be picked up. A lapel mic is a great way to combat this and focus purely on your voice, as are USB microphones.

A hot tip on mics: make sure nothing is rubbing against them!

Finally, make sure you record in a room that doesn't have an echo—carpeted rooms are best, or you can place towels or blankets against the walls to absorb unwanted sound and echoes. Failing that, wardrobes are great places for recording! Failing that, wardrobes are a great place for recording audio.

Viewing yourself

Make sure you look at yourself in the mirror before recording, put on about ten per cent more makeup than you usually would (matte is best), and tidy up any wispy pieces of hair. Wear earrings that don't distract attention, jewellery that doesn't jingle, and clothing that won't rub too easily on a mic—you don't want anything to distract viewers from your message.

Check on your internal self
Shake out any nerves, put on some pumping music and really up your vibe. The camera turns us from 3D beings into 2D beings, so we are losing ten per cent of our normal self. Give yourself a ten per cent boost when it comes to your energy and also nourish yourself before you go on camera (just make sure you check your teeth).

Do a trial run
Lastly, before you hit record, you'll want to have tested everything. Test the visual, the audio and the screen share (if you're using this function), and take three deep breaths.

Your first deep breath comes all the way in and goes all the way out; it grounds you and connects you to the earth—because trust me, you'll be in your head!

The next deep breath connects you with your audience—you want to make sure that you have a golden trail between you and the people that need to hear your message.

The third breath connects you with your purpose: the reason you're sharing this message in the first place.

Once you've done that, hit the record button, share your message and, at the end, review and replay it to make sure that you haven't got any issues—technical or otherwise.

And lastly, remember that it doesn't have to be perfect. You showing up for the people you need to get your message to is way more important than all the fancy extra stuff. Make sure that you share from your heart, and that you're sharing in such a direct way that the person on the other end is motivated to start taking the actions you're asking them to take.

Challenge
Start being seen!

It's time to record that video, whether it's a welcome for your business, an introduction to you and your ebook, or an explanation of the first modules of your e-course. Or even just practise by doing live videos on socials and giving these tips a go.

"

Structure
enables
flexibility.

Chapter 7
Money

 Rule: You have to work hard for your money and be afraid of losing it

Fuel: Money can be fun and knowing your numbers is empowering

In the space of three years, I met the love of my life, became a step-parent, finished my naturopathic degree, completed my pathology career, got engaged and then married, had a baby and started my business.

My new hubby, Murray, owned his own house and had a stable corporate career, just as my parents did. At the time, I thought the guy looked after the money and I kind of had 'play money'. In the first twelve months of my business, I thought I was being all grown up with all the adult things, but looking back I was really running a hobby, not taking it seriously and spending a lot of money.

My nervous system was also going through a LOT. Juggling three kids, a blended family and my identity as a new wife and mother was plenty to have on my plate. Add into the mix a new business and all the stresses that come with that, and I was starting to feel incredibly overwhelmed.

One night, after we finished dinner, I decided to run a bubble bath to try to wind down. I was sitting in the bathroom waiting for the bubbles to rise when Murray came in with our credit card statement in hand. The moment I saw it, my heart froze. The colours of the letterhead matched my business credit card—the one whose upper limit I secretly increased about a month ago, and had already maxed out.

The one I hadn't told Murray about.

The five-figure debt that he didn't know about … it was in his hands in black and white.

I burst out crying, sobbing by the bath. For the longest time, I couldn't find the words.

I had no idea how to even talk about money, or the struggles of being in that office alone, day in, day out. I had no idea where to even start with this whole business thing.

Since then, I've been committed to financial literacy, learning through books, courses and coaches and applying everything I can. More importantly, Murray and I have a whole new level of communication when it comes to money. We share insights from books we've read; we changed the set-up of our business accounts, employed financial advisors, accountants and bookkeepers; and regularly meet to set clear goals and go over the numbers. I now find conversations about numbers and money some of the most empowering we can have.

This is one of the most important and empowering chapters in this book, so make sure you go all-in on this one. We will be looking at both the logical and metaphysical side of money, creating the money we want—and the big one for many practitioners out there—how to actually price your offerings.

Money and numbers are some of the most interesting and emotionally charged things that we come across as business owners.

There have been moments when money and numbers cause me to unravel. No matter where you are in business, you are not immune. But when you think about it, you need to separate the facts from the meanings when it comes to numbers and financial situations. The fact is that numbers are simply a way to measure something.

In the case of numbers—all of our clients, followers and products—they're just a measuring tool.

Money is also a form of measurement, because it can measure whatever it is we aspire to—whether that's wealth, success or security.

I invite you to come to this with an open mind. Check with awareness what is coming up for you—including emotions and self-talk—when we start to talk about money and numbers.

You can make heaps of money

Learning how to be a naturopath didn't give me the skills to run a business and make money. After a while, I realised that I needed to educate myself about business. Once I had done that, my income started to grow as well.

Money doesn't have to be a dirty word.

Everyone has the ability to make money and create abundance.

I have witnessed business owners go from being on food handouts one month to earning $60,000 the next by realigning their business and selling an incredible course about their experience in a structured way that got results.

I've also seen a newly qualified practitioner and business owner make $220,000 a year working one day a week of client-facing hours. She did this by creating a program that served even more people, so she could take care of her special needs family members and pay off her mortgage.

I've seen service providers take the time to create one course and then build their audience to a point where they have six-figure course launches every time.

I hear these stories all the time, and I wish they were shared more freely rather than in hushed tones.

There are two reasons we don't hear these stories:

1. The shared brule (conscious or subconscious) that we shouldn't be helping people to get rich.
2. Because tall poppy syndrome is rife in the business world. When someone excels at what they do, the competition kicks in rather than collaboration or celebration. None of us wants to be ostracised from the tribe—we want to belong.

You can lose heaps of money too

Brule: It's all about the endgame. Nothing will work unless you have big numbers.

Fuel: All journeys start with a single step, a single person, a single like. Start where you are at.

Don't be scared to have the right conversation with the right people. If you're not doing well in your business, talk to an expert. Knowing your numbers is empowering once you move through the fear of looking at them in the first place.

The first time I found out that I was in five-figure debt was when I finally handed over my shoebox of unopened bills and receipts to a bookkeeper, who, after popping everything into a spreadsheet for me, told me it was time to see an accountant.

It had taken two years of me being too afraid to open the bills because, well, I knew 'around about' what was in there and 'around about' what I had been spending, and that 'the clients would flow in soon'. As soon as my husband had walked in with that credit card statement, I realised it was time to take action—and I couldn't do it on my own.

At the time, I thought moving through that issue and clearing my debt was the be-all and end-all of learning about money. But the truth is, no matter where you are on your entrepreneurial journey, there are always more lessons.

One Friday afternoon at my clinic, a sales rep came around with 'an offer I couldn't refuse.' He worked for a website that worked with businesses to offer discount vouchers for their services to get new clients.

Did I want more clients? Well, yes of course.

'Then create an offer so low that everyone will want to buy it,' he said.

With the coaxing of the sales rep, I decided to sell my one-hour massages for half price at $35 an hour. Over the next four weeks, 104 people bought those massages, and I thought I had hit the jackpot.

As the 'clients' started to come in, reality set in; they weren't the type of clients to come back. And of those 104, 1 converted into a naturopathic client. The rest basically disappeared.

Sitting alone at my desk in the practically abandoned building where I had my first clinic room, I was watching an online training video about 'How to run a webinar and get one hundred people'. I decided that all my years as a trainer at Cadets and a coach at gymnastics, and some of the adult learning I had done, could be put to good use in sharing my knowledge of the human body on a grander scale.

I made the most extraordinary PowerPoint presentation. I poured my heart and head into that presentation. I had those one hundred people that the training told me to get in my mind when I was creating it. I stayed up after my kids went to bed. I even had animations.

I learned how to use the suggested webinar platform, and as the day came closer, I had a grand total of thirteen sign-ups (including some of my clients and friends that I had invited). Although thirteen was a far cry from the one hundred people that the training told me I should aim for, I was pretty chuffed.

The morning of the webinar, I was super early to work, nervously scrolling through my slides and checking the internet. I'm not a makeup gal, but I definitely went a notch further than I usually do … to get that 'professional' look. The clock ticked down and I started recording. I looked at the number of live participants … zero. I made small talk for a couple of minutes … still zero. *Is the software working? What if no one shows up? There are supposed to be one hundred … and I thought thirteen was bad … now there's ZERO.*

In that moment I had a choice. I could consider myself the failure my mind believed me to be due to all the brules I had bought into … or I could start where I was at.

I presented the bejesus out of that PowerPoint … to absolutely no one. I even answered questions at the end that I had prepared earlier.

I sent out the recording to the thirteen people. Three wrote lovely messages back saying how informative it was. One booked in with me and became one of my longest-running clients.

Facts versus meaning

If we think about numbers as they are—1, 2, 3, 4, 5—do any of these actually create an emotional response? Do you feel triggered or inspired if we talk about the number one or the number six? Probably not; they are simply numbers. It is the *meaning* we place on numbers that we need to be aware of.

The same thing applies when we talk about one hundred versus one thousand versus one million: it is the context, not the content, that we attach meaning to. If we are comparing $100 to $1 million, then different emotions start to come to the surface due to the different meanings that we create.

> *Oh, I can do a hundred dollars. But a million dollars— no way!*
>
> *My parents never made a million dollars.*
>
> *People with a million dollars have so many problems—I wouldn't want to have a million dollars because of the million issues that come with it.*

Alternatively, your meaning could be more positive. Perhaps making a million dollars is one of the most freeing things you could ever do and you aspire to it.

Can you see that numbers are simply numbers? They are a numerical measuring tool; it is the meaning we make out of them that creates how we feel about them.

A better way to look at numbers

In another instance, numbers could measure popularity. The number of followers you have on social media, or the number of people who are following your business—we can attribute a popularity meaning to it. The more numbers we have, the more important we are; the more money we have, the more important we are; the more followers we have, the more important we are.

Is that really the case? Does it also mean that because I have fewer clients than somebody else, I am somehow a lesser practitioner than them? Because I have more clients or more time than somebody else, am I better than them?

We need to simply replace those thoughts. What if the amount of money given to you, the numbers in the form of money, is actually energy?

> I gave that person $20 worth of energy and they're giving me $20 worth of energy back.

> I created $100 worth of joy for this person and then they gave me $100 worth of joy back.

We could think of money as joy tokens: I gave them joy, and they gave me joy tokens back so I can spend them on things that bring me joy.

What if we thought about money as a measure of gratitude or value? We can create value for others, and they give us the value back in the form of this special token money.

> I gave them $100 worth of gratitude for being able to express my gift, talents and knowledge, and they've given me the gratitude tokens back.

I can then give the gratitude tokens to somebody who is going to give me a holiday, which I'll feel grateful for. I can exchange the gratitude tokens for food and the amazing nutrients that I can get.

Maybe for you it's contribution—what if we contribute the equivalent of $160 to somebody's life and their health, and they give us $160 worth of contribution tokens back? Then we're going to contribute to our feelings and joy through travel, for example. We could contribute to our family, our home, or even our community.

Start paying attention

The next step in exploring your money mindset revolves around the concept that *where your attention goes, your energy flows.*

Have you had your head in the sand around your money? You're not alone. But when you don't pay any attention to your money, it can diminish—just like your plants if you're not paying them any attention.

It's time to stop hiding and allow your energy and attention to flow towards your money.

When we consider the law of attraction, we are talking about where we are spending our time and energy, which is similar to spending and receiving money. If we talk about focusing our energies on a subconscious level, then we're talking about the reticular activating system. This system allows our brain to focus in on something and identify its patterns. Once the brain recognises its pattern, it then goes on to find more patterns similar to it.

When we start to focus our attention on money, then energy

starts to flow to that area.

Start focusing your attention on money coming in.

A great way to bring attention to your money is to track it. Let's explore what happens when you track every dollar that comes in over a week.

What's coming in

Start with everything that is coming in (not what is going out):

- gifts and gift cards
- found money in your pockets or furniture
- deposits into your spare accounts, including PayPal
- any cheques you haven't banked
- unexpected refunds
- affiliate payments
- the usual wages
- client payments

Track it, write it down and celebrate.

It is very easy to notice the bills we have—we are hardwired to notice money that's going *out*. This only reinforces the notion of where your attention goes, energy flows, and you may notice more places where money goes out.

In reality, there is always going to be money going out, but this is a practice about attracting money. Remember, where attention goes, energy flows, and we want that energy flowing in.

Track it all for a month

Track everything, both personal and business, for a month. Track the incoming money and celebrate. Feel grateful for every dollar: every dollar is a gratitude, joy or contribution token. The money coming in is something that has been given in exchange for your value.

Once you have been tracking like this for a month, your reticular activating system starts to see what's going on and notices the patterns.

Manifest and create

Look at opportunities to manifest and create. Every single day that you're tracking every dollar that is coming into your world, there is an opportunity to have an abundant mindset and create a relationship with the money coming in—a relationship built on gratitude.

You may also like to write an affirmation at the top of your recorded incomings that focuses on easily and joyfully attracting money into your life.

We need to hone in on our gratitude for things coming in, rather than only noticing the things going out.

Making a profit

Your incomings provide an amazing opportunity to practise gratitude for what you have created in the world and what is flowing to you. But we also have the outgoings—they are all the things that you have to spend money on to keep your business running, to keep you running, and to keep everything going. When the incomings are equal to outgoings, this is the break-even point.

When you are making money from your meetings, online offerings, products, training or any other way you attract it, then you then have to spend it on your outgoings. Your outgoings can be anything from your electricity and water bills, to your rent, websites, online subscriptions and postage costs, as well as your future anticipated outgoings. When it comes to manifesting and focusing on how money is coming in and going out, you have to be really specific about wanting to achieve more than just the break-even point.

Trust me, I went through this for years, hitting break-even in my business because I was only focusing on what it took to keep my business going: the incomings and outgoings. I didn't focus on what the contribution could be to my family and my life.

What we are talking about here is creating *profit*—what comes in on top of the break-even point. With profit, you can start to save money and contribute to yourself, your family, your goals and your aspirations, as well as create a growth pocket for your business in the future so you can expand and scale.

Money in, money out, profit—these are the real basics of business building and there are many books focusing on these, but I wanted to introduce a mindset for these so you can begin to see them through a different lens.

The horizons

One of my favourite ways to think about our money and business goals is using horizon one, horizon two and horizon three. I live near the beach and I fly helicopters. As we set our goal on the horizon, there are a number of things we need to take care of before we get to it.

Horizon one
When we are on the beach looking out to the horizon, the truth is, our human eyes and the shape of the earth only allow us to see about ten kilometres ahead. From this angle, we can really only see the next wave rolling in, then we have to brace ourselves

for the next one. When we're in the water, we can't see what's beneath the surface, so there is always a sense of uncertainty, often combined with a recurrent sense of overwhelm in keeping our head above water. If we take our eyes off the waves, there is a tendency to go under.

It's difficult to see the path when we're looking at horizon one. To truly see it, we need resources, like a boat, to reach it. Horizon one is associated with a survival feeling.

Horizon two
A helicopter or lighthouse can give us the next level of perspective. There are a number of steps to be taken to utilise these resources: experiences to be had, or knowledge to acquire. But from a higher vantage point we can see that the horizon goes further; things we couldn't have imagined before appear in the distance, and we start to see the larger rhythm at play with the waves and potential hazards. We can also see opportunities when they arise.

Horizon three
If again we take further steps to go to the next level, whether it is up to the top of the lighthouse or even higher in a helicopter, horizon three allows us to see even further. The appearance of islands or other ships in the distance creates a fuller picture of our place in the world and how we can not only make the most of the prevailing conditions, but how we can better contribute to the whole.

Towards the top we can see the whole landscape—the sunrise, the sunset, the clouds, the atmosphere—and how that can all change the ocean.

Each level requires different skills, as things on the bottom level might not work the same way at the top level.

If you recognise that you might be on the survival level, then there are three really useful things you can do to get out.

One of them is measuring your money now. It's easy to put your head in the sand, but if you don't pay any attention to where you're at right now, then your energy can't be redirected to getting you where you want to be.

The next thing is committing to checking in with your money daily and building it into a positive experience rather than a negative one.

The third thing is doing your duty—showing up and getting things done. Stop spending money you don't have, work when you have the opportunity, and be consistent and purposeful.

In order to get to horizon two and then three, there is a different set of things you will need to do. Surviving is about breaking even rather than drowning, whereas going for horizon two is about working hard for your money. You get the money because you showed up for work, and you can cover your expenses and have a little bit left over for holidays and such.

The way to move up is to consistently refine your passion: find what feels authentic for you, what lights you up, what you want to save money for.

Then set your standards—what will you or won't you put up with? Are you going to put up with constantly having $10 left in your bank account, or do you want $100 or $1000 left over? Set your new standard and don't go below it.

The next thing to do is follow the flow—cash comes in and out of our lives. Just as we can follow the waves, rips and currents from the lighthouse, we can follow the flow of money in our lives.

In order to go after horizon three, you'll need to identify what makes you unique and create structures that work while you are not there, through automation, delegation or elimination. Similar to having the light at the top of the lighthouse, these support systems amplify what you can do and get you to your goal more efficiently and effectively.

My horizons concept was influenced by Roger James Hamilton's Wealth Lighthouse, which I recommend looking up.

Do your duty

Rule: You can run a business by the seat of your pants

Fuel: Hobbies are run by the seat of your pants; business is built on solid foundations

It's one thing to have a hobby, but it's another to run a business. The conversations with my accountant about this in the early stages of my business were very challenging! It's so important to get clear with integrity and commitment from the beginning that you will be running a business.

This means you've got to put your big business pants on. It means that you need to make sure that you are crossing your T's and dotting your I's—getting your legals in place, along with your insurance, business registration, tax and other things that we all have a tendency to push aside.

It's time to really take it seriously and see what you can take action on. Make sure you have all of the foundational things in place from which to build.

Chapter 8
Flow

Bhule: You work hard for your money, and the way you think about it won't change how much you can get

Fuel: Change your mind around money, change your life

For money to flow into your business, we need to remove obstacles in your income stream. This isn't only about money coming in, but also about not fearing the expenses that come with running a business, and investments that could help you to reach higher.

This may be a section that you keep coming back to, whether you're at the very beginning or hitting a whole new level in business. You will come across money 'blocks' and other interesting ideas about money, and I'll let you in on a little secret: unfortunately, they don't go away.

So, it's really good to get the tools in this section down pat before you even begin.

My friend and money-mindset coach Denise Duffield-Thomas has authored some fantastic books and articles on this exact topic. Money blocks are something to take seriously, and working through them takes time and effort.

Many of us, myself included, have had money stories handed down to us from generations back—but are they outdated?

Three generations back, our ancestors were going through the Great Depression. Two generations back, they were going through war. And one generation back—my parent's generation—they were in the middle of the working-class industrial age.

Right now, we are living in a very different society, but often we believe old money stories that aren't exactly applicable to us now. It's like trying to run old software on a new computer or phone.

I want you to explore and take the time to consider all of the money stories and memories that you've had in your head from as far back as you can remember. Think about your earliest stories to do with money, or a lack thereof, and write them down.

One of mine was: *You've got to work hard for your money.* I had to overcome this one, because what if I created a passive income stream by sharing my knowledge without even needing to sit across from a one-on-one client?

Seeing one-on-one clients *is* working hard—I have to be there, I have to be present, and I have to give up some of my time. On the other hand, passive income, such as an e-course, means I only have to create the content once and people get value from it over and over again. But because I don't have to be there, it doesn't feel like hard work.

This was a real money block for me when I was first starting out.

Exercise
Forgiveness is a superpower

Once you've got your stories, I want you to go back over each one. I want you to use these four phrases from the Hawaiian affirmation called hoʻoponopono: *I'm sorry, please forgive me, thank you, I love you.*

I'm sorry—for the role that I played in that story. And I'm sorry for buying into that story.

I forgive you—for having these stories because they very likely came from a situation or generation before. I forgive myself for the part I played in that story.

Thank you—for the lesson that you have taught me and everything I've learned from it.

Forgiveness is one of the biggest things that we can do for each of the stories, especially when we can feel it in a part of our body.

And lastly, *I love you*: so many of those stories come from loved ones, and it creates a real vibrational shift when we can actually get to a place of forgiveness and loving those moments, because they gave us an important lesson and experience that help to move us forward.

Please take the time to do this exercise and lean into the feelings the stories bring up. If you get stuck, write a forgiveness letter.

This exercise is powerful, and if you don't do it, it can trip you up when the time comes to put out new offerings or prices.

The art of collecting money

Rule: If they find out how much it is, it will always be too much

Fuel: Clarity is kindness

Collecting money is a normal part of business and it is really one of the biggest things that we as practitioners can get tripped up over at the last minute. I should know! In the beginning, when I had my first clients, I'd spend way more time with them than what was scheduled—sometimes ninety minutes instead of sixty. At the end of the consultation, I'd prepare the EFTPOS machine and blurt out, 'Oh, it is fifty per cent off today!' Crazy, right?

Most of us experience this—or some version of it—at some point in our careers. This is why it is super important to be clear on your prices, remove past any money blocks, and be paid what you set out to be paid.

There are three different ways to set prices.

- From your head—which is often influenced by how other practitioners are setting their prices.
- From the heart—choosing the amount that you truly feel is what you deserve for your time and expertise. It's what you feel comfortable charging your clients, knowing they will still feel like they're getting the best value for money.
- From your gut—that space between your mind and heart.

Setting prices is a personal thing and there is no right or wrong way to do it, but you need to land on a price and share it with your audience—put it on your website, and send out a newsletter with your updated pricing structure. Making sure other people know your prices makes you more accountable for ensuring you are correctly and fairly paid every time.

Follow through with it. Charge that amount of money, receive it and say thank you. Lean in.

Removing the obstacles to buying from you

I recently went to book a flight, and the process was terrible. I placed in all the details, filled out extra questions that weren't even relevant, and then it wouldn't even work on my phone. I then tried to call the airline and couldn't get through.

So I went to another provider instead—two clicks later, my ticket was booked.

Although it cost me $15 extra, it was so simple, it didn't take up all of my time, it didn't take any more effort and I didn't have to fill in any random forms. It was so much easier because there were no obstacles in the way for me to buy that flight.

What are the potential obstacles for your ideal client when they see you on social media, on your website, or in person? What could get in the way of them buying from you?

There are a few general barriers to buying that I learned about from being in business for a decade and serving thousands of people.

Obstacle one: *It's too expensive at the moment*
This one is not an actual fact for a lot of people. It's not necessarily expensive; it's more likely that they haven't seen the value in it yet.

This barrier comes up a lot, particularly when we haven't clearly relayed to people the value of what we are offering in their lives.

Most often, clients have come from the medical model, so they don't always recognise the value of what we can create for them.

They're going to spend the same amount of money on their car or on having their hair done, but when it comes to their health, often we have to explain to them the *value* of spending that money. They need to understand what they're going to get in return to see that it's of benefit.

We want to make sure that they've been educated on the value we can provide, how many times they may need to come back, and approximately how much it will cost with the consultations and remedies.

This could easily reach a couple of thousand dollars, which is hard to pay upfront—this is why payment plans are great and very easy to set up.

Consider the way this value comes across to your client—$2,000 all up, or $200 per week for the next ten weeks.

Which option sounds more doable?

When you offer a payment plan, make sure that you explain the benefits they're getting at the end of those ten weeks.

It may be that at the end of the ten weeks they'll have their IBS sorted, the freedom to move around without worrying where the toilets are, fifty per cent more energy and better quality sleep.

Whatever the most likely outcome is at the end of the given timeframe, make sure they know about it!

Obstacle two: *I can't book in*

They've been calling and can't get a hold of you. We all get busy, not all of us can afford a receptionist, and it's hard to get around to the answering machine when we're under the pump. The best and easiest way to get around this obstacle is by having an online booking system. This allows the client to book in at midnight on a Sunday when they are freaking out about their health issue. It removes the barrier of waiting and captures them when they feel the most motivated to book.

The other benefit is that it allows people to see when you are available and choose a time that suits both parties. You can even close off some of your appointment availabilities so it doesn't look like you have no one booked in.

Another great benefit of an online booking system is that if you get audited, your records are clearly organised and stored—try to find in a flipbook or paper diary where and when you last saw a particular client, whether they were a no-show, whether they rebooked, or whether you have connected with them recently. It can be a mission!

When being audited, they can request to review particular clients across a period of seven years. Having an online, searchable record of all the details is sanity saving, to say the least.

There are many booking systems out there—just google 'online booking system' and your profession to find one appropriate for you.

Obstacle three: *I don't know what to book*

This one often comes up if you have a lot of different options (such as different appointment lengths), or a variety of packages that may not be clear to potential clients. What they're really saying is, *I am ready to spend money with you, but I don't know what to buy.*

So, focus on the benefits over explanations:

- Instead of: 'You will get sixty minutes of my time and a report.'
- Go with: 'This particular package will have you feeling more energetic, sleeping better and experiencing less anxiety.'

Also, be sure not to give them more than three options that would suit them—reduce the decision fatigue!

Obstacle four: *It takes too long*
If you ever use Audible or Amazon, you'll notice that you can literally buy a book using one button that says 'Buy this book in one click'. So, instead of having your client click through to X page, then choose their payment method, then put their card details in, then confirm, and so on, you could have a more simplified 'one click to book' button.

Obstacle five: *I don't have enough time*
This obstacle comes from a lack of education around what the client is investing their time in. They have enough time to take their kids to school and to sports, and clean the house. So they obviously need educating either via a blog, audio recording, diagram, or even an infographic about where their time can be better spent on themselves and their health in the long run.

I don't have enough time to do your program. I don't have enough time to come to the one-hour initial consultation. How will I have enough time to commit to these three months to get my health back on track?

Again, it's about education. We have to show up consistently to educate people and that's the bit we tend to miss.

Obstacle six: *I'm not local to you*
Ideal clients want to see the practitioner that is ideal to them, regardless of location. So, how can you create a one-click way to connect with you via Skype, Zoom, or phone? And once you have connected with them, now is the opportunity to offer them your e-course. Make it easy for them to access you and your message.

The obvious benefit of offering virtual appointments is that it widens your customer base globally.

A note here on not stretching yourself too thin—I know entrepreneurs who are awake almost twenty-four hours to offer services to people in different time zones. It's important to have boundaries, even when you want to help people across the world.

Doing something for nothing

Eighteen months into my business, I felt like I had lost sight of the whole purpose of doing it all. I'd moved premises twice, and I felt like I couldn't see more than a couple of clients a week. I had recently done a six-month Women in Business program, a state-subsidised business mentoring program that had me thinking about all the spreadsheets, profit and loss, and the acquisition of leads. My head was full of business, business, business.

The pendulum had swung from being neck deep in the biology and psychology of helping humans, to an ever-increasing list of what I was supposed to do to be a success in business. And somewhere in the middle there I was a relatively new mum and wife.

It was a beautiful autumn morning and I was at my Kmart desk in the serviced office I had rented in the city. It looked out over an abandoned sandstone post office building, but had a massive tree in front of it, with the leaves slowly yellowing and turning the footpath golden.

It was a time before social media was popular, but I was in an internet-search spiral. I found myself typing in 'volunteer naturopath'. I knew I couldn't afford to go anywhere too far, but I knew I needed to get away.

In my mind at the time, I didn't think I could justify to my husband that I needed a week away, just for me.

After thoroughly exploring the possibility of volunteering in Guatemala, I stumbled on a clinic on Aore Island in Vanuatu. This clinic was run by an Australian couple who also had a sailing charter. They ran a clinic in Brisbane too but went to Vanuatu regularly. I emailed immediately to find out when their next window would be, and sure enough it was in a month's time.

Freedom being my highest value, I've never found myself more motivated than when having an adventure is the outcome.

By the end of that month, I had made exactly the amount required to cover the cost of the tickets and pay for the little bure on the island.

After arriving at Aore Island and being greeted by Alan and his gorgeous wife, Deb, I settled into the bure cabin and I perceptibly felt my nervous system relax. The tropical breeze, the smell of the ocean mixed with frangipanis at sunset, and the sound of chickens clucking and the water lapping just down from my cabin lulled me into a deep sleep.

The following morning as I explored the clinic with Alan, he shared stories of befriending the local community, the struggles of teaching them about the evils of sugar and rice (not native to their diet of yams and fresh fruit), as well as the way the salt air aged equipment before it was used, and the islanders' shared love of God. Although I don't consider myself religious, I could see the sacredness with which he held this bond and I was moved by it.

After lunch I helped Deb with the dispensary, a hodgepodge of natural medicines gifted by Australian clinics and companies to help the local community. I was apprehensive about the following day but tinkering with herbs, supplements and stethoscopes was a purposeful distraction.

That evening as the sun set, I was walking along the thin line of sand on the beach, being cautious to avoid the coral, whilst enamoured by the full moon.

I remember sitting on a massive piece of driftwood underneath a bent-over palm tree, watching hermit crabs scuttle across the sand—the epitome of an island dream. I wished to see the stars and the moon: *I'm here. I have all these gifts and talents. I am totally ready for my next step; just point me in the right direction and I will dive in one hundred per cent.*

A fish jumped out of the water, and I jumped in. I fully submerged myself, and I am certain I came out of the water a different woman to the one who went in.

The following day started early, with people arriving from 7:00 am from neighbouring islands by longboat and tinny. Whole families walked across Aore to take their numbered ticket and sit on the sloped lawn out the front of the clinic, under the shade of the massive fig trees.

There were seventy-six tickets taken that day and Alan saw every last one. They patiently waited their turn, talking in hushed tones to 'Dr Alan', as they called him. And I watched as he took their vitals, penned notes, asked questions with direct eye contact, and held their hands as they prayed to 'Papa God' at the end of every consult for continued good health for themselves and those they loved.

They were then directed to the dispensary, where myself and Deb were stationed. We took their file and made up twelve weeks' worth of remedies for them.

Part of the process was to listen to an educational session at midday under the trees, and then they could go. It was here that the most basic nutrition and public health knowledge was imparted, but I wasn't to know the true impact of this until we came back many years after.

By the end of the day, I was pooped, but I was also euphoric. I felt like I had contributed in a very real way. What's more, I felt like so many more natural health practitioners needed to know this feeling. I knew I needed to bring them here—to be reminded of why they began this journey in the first place.

That trip has stayed with me, and without a doubt changed the way I run my business. Yes, money is important and should be part of your aspirations, but there's also a lot to be gained from using your gifts and your skill sets pro bono, in small or large ways.

You don't have to go to another country and join a volunteer organisation to do it. It could be deciding to give two scholarships a year, running a giveaway for a free session at a time when you know people are financially struggling, or taking the time to mentor someone coming up behind you in your industry.

Looking back, the trip gave me a sense of resourcefulness and reminded me of how powerful working for yourself can be.

"

Where your
attention goes,
energy flows.

Chapter 9
Magic

Rule: Success should just happen in my business

Fuel: I'm excited to help make the magic happen

As a practitioner, I believe in the healing power of nature and 'life force'—principles passed down from our forebears in natural health. I have grown very used to the effects of unseen forces in my personal and family life.

The magic of WHO
The magic of WHAT
The magic of WHEN
The magic of HOW

This magic occurs in business too. Whether it's the energy of a conversation or the vibe of procrastination, we have to identify these forces and have strategies to work with them. We all have moments in our business where we feel like miracles and magic happen—and these are incredible moments, but they're also not passive events. We all have a role to play—as entrepreneurs, business owners, and healers—to create a business where magic can flow more easily.

So, this chapter is all about looking at the strategies and systems you can put in place to make room for miracles—and remove the hurdles that are holding you back.

This is where real magic and next-level strategy meet. And it's an exciting step to take. You have big plans and big dreams. Don't be scared to tell people about them. You will become known as the person who does 'that thing'.

Even if you fail, you will be much further ahead than anyone who hasn't even tried.

We can all help heal the world

Rule: Nothing I do makes a difference anyway

Fuel: I have the capacity to change people's lives in ways I can't even imagine

The first step in welcoming magic into your business is really believing in yourself. Of course, it's a theme throughout the book, but now it's time to really step into your power. We are all here to heal something for our clients and customers, whether it's a health issue, a stress point in their family life, a problem with their kid's childcare, or an issue with their technology that is dragging them down.

Imagine the change you can create in someone's life from just one hour-long conversation in your practice. Having the right conversation at the right moment may just be the catalyst someone needs.

I was invited to the funeral of a long-term client of mine. He and his wife ran one of the most amazing drycleaners in town.

He came to me wanting to lose a bit of weight, through a cancer diagnosis, through losing his leg and all the mental and emotional turmoil that goes with that.

The conversations we had about life—their bucket-list trips, their award-winning business that became known for its inclusion of disabled staff, and, of course, food, herbs and health—will always be in my memories.

Another client had been told she was unable to have children due to a polycystic ovarian syndrome diagnosis. In a sixty-minute appointment, I shared how reproduction actually works, explained her pathology results to her and let her know the simple foods and herbs that could assist her. We also set a goal of her going on a romantic holiday away from her stressful job.

Within three months, she was pregnant. She didn't think she would ever have a family. She had grieved a life she wouldn't have. Then she got it.

I'll forever remember a seven-year-old who came and saw me who had rubbed her nose down to the cartilage with night itches. She could only fall asleep with an icepack on her nose. She cried herself to sleep every night. Her poor mum was at her wits' end.

We discussed how the body works, what types of things our bodies generally get itchy from, and explored what might be in her diet and her home that was causing it.

Then we talked about things that could help, drawing on my training in biochemistry, homeopathy and nutrition. I expected it to take some time, as it was quite severe.

Six weeks later, she and her mum came back and, to my utter surprise, when I asked her how she had been sleeping, she said, 'Awesome.' She didn't even remember the last time she used the icepack.

These are just some of the amazing memories I have from my practice, and you will have some too no matter what industry you're in. This is the magic of following your passions and talents, and working from the heart.

When we apply what we have learned, with an intention to do our best for the person in front of us, all kinds of magic occur.

The one bad thing

We've all been there. You're on a winning streak, or so it feels. Your business is expanding, your kids haven't had a cold in months, your relationship is harmonious, you've got so much to be thankful for. And then one bad day or bad thing happens— and it's all you can think about. It's overshadowed all of the light that's around you.

It can happen very easily in your business, because as entrepreneurs we're hypersensitive to criticism (it's our business baby after all!). You are sailing along and life is good. Then all of a sudden you get a review or feedback that is not so great. Despite the millions of emails you get that are really positive, it can really pull you down. And that is okay to admit! We're all only human after all.

I've been there. Whether it is a querulous complainer, a competitor with a grudge, or something random that seemingly comes out of the blue, there are three main points I follow.

1. Opportunities for improvement

There are lessons to learn in these situations; we can't just smooth it over immediately. Often when these things come out of the blue, they bring our attention to something we were already concerned about ourselves. Something that hadn't quite made it to the top of the to-do list. And now that it's been brought to our attention, we are kicking ourselves we didn't do it earlier.

I've had this with branding, when I'm launching a new service or product. Suddenly, a competitor comes out with the tagline I hadn't had the chance to yet.

I've had it with a request for a refund, when I hadn't got around to updating my refund policy.

Instead of beating yourself up for procrastinating or seeing the complaint as 'evil', it's about changing your mindset. These moments give you a chance to improve your business and your operations—to tighten up something you had been meaning to get to all along.

2. Upper limits

The phrase 'upper limit' is coined from the book *The Big Leap* by Gay Hendricks. In it, he outlines an invisible energetic barrier that we tend to push ourselves up against when we are striving for a new level. As we get close to living a life we haven't lived before, something happens that jolts us into staying the same.

This used to happen to me when I had the opportunity to do speaking gigs. I would lose my voice or come down with a cold just before the event and I wouldn't be able to do it.

Another upper limit I often see with clients is triggered by social media trolls. Just as we feel confident enough to take our message out to the world, the keyboard warriors appear out of nowhere to test our resolve.

The last upper limit that many of us experience is financial. As we move into a position where more money becomes available, something substantial breaks down—a car, a washing machine—and we have to find a new way through.

The good news is, upper limits show that a new level is available to us and it's much closer than we think.

3. Celebrate the bad stuff as much as the good

Often these bumps in the road are nudges in the right direction that we can only see with the benefit of hindsight. Celebrating that our message has reached an audience big enough to get a troll is awesome. Celebrating someone else's gift in the grammatical arts allows our newsletters to become better and better.

When some asks for a refund, have a little inner party—it means there is going to be room for more aligned customers in your world. Give yourself a pat on the back for completing those niggling actions on your to-do list. It's a wonderful mindset to have for the longevity of your business.

Eat that frog (eliminate procrastination)

Rule: I have to nail it every day; ticking off a to-do list is ultimate success

Fuel: Work smarter not harder

You know the feeling where, just before your eyes open for the day, you see your to-do list, you envision yourself nailing it—answering emails, following up with clients, getting on top of your finances and orders, marketing like a mofo and sending off that newsletter—and then another voice pops in suggesting you need coffee first, and to clean up your desk, and light a candle … and then before you know it, another day disappears and the to-do list is actually longer than it was to begin with.

This is one of the reasons I love the 'eat the frog' way of planning your day—the idea that you should do the job you least want to do first and then save the more palatable tasks for afterwards. This concept comes from the book *Eat that Frog!* by Brian Tracy, and it's one of the best tools I've found for doing the things you need to do and avoiding procrastination. The premise of the book is based on Mark Twain's quote, 'Eat a live frog early in the morning and nothing worse will happen to you the rest of the day.'

So, how can you action it? Well, what's that thing on your to-do list that you've been ignoring because it feels slimy and weird and yucky? Give yourself a moment to check out your to-do list, and apply a priority to it.

- For me, the most important items get a green highlighter; in business, the most important areas for keeping the doors open are finances and clients. I will often have bills, bookings, and phone calls to make to people who pay me. Also included here are urgent things of high consequence that need to be attended to now.

- Next, I get the orange highlighter for things that are urgent but not as important; things that may be holding up bigger projects, or expanding timelines that have no immediate effect on me, but could be critical to a team effort.

- Yellow highlighter items are my 'nice to dos', but are of little consequence. These may include a new ebook or handout, or free training.

- Pink highlighter items are for delegation; they can be done by others. These tasks often find their way to the bottom of the list anyway, and take someone else a lot less time to do them. In my world, these are things like turning my blog articles into newsletters, updating my website, or making something more visually beautiful.

I like to think I can do these things, but they would be easier and quicker for someone else to do, and delegating them would free up time for me to do the green, orange and yellow tasks.

If you have tasks left over, consider if they need to be eliminated; perhaps they are the result of old ideas, habits or tools that take you away from more important work, and can simply be let go of.

I'm not saying that 'slimy' task will suddenly be enjoyable—it's still probably going to be yucky, but you're going to do it anyway. As soon as you actually eat that frog, it will be shifted, and you'll be able to do things more easily, cleanly and quickly for the rest of the day.

Sharing wisely

One of those 'magical forces' that I've seen hold back many a practitioner or entrepreneur from sharing is: how much do I share? How deep do I go with each of my clients? How deep do I go with the information I'm putting in my ebook or e-course?

If you've spent years, and even decades, training in a specialist subject, you can feel like you're doing your clients a disservice but not sharing ALL OF IT! The truth is, however, that different clients want different levels of information, and overwhelming them can be the first step to losing them.

This is the space to create an awareness of where you might need to give more information, and where you might actually need to give less. It comes down to being really aware of your client's needs, but also your own capacity; you have to share in a sustainable way for you too—a way that allows you to rest and restore your reserves.

The pyramid of information

When we're sharing information in our online offerings, what we're trying to do is match the expectations of our target market. Our ideal client needs to know a certain amount of information in order to be able to retain it and then move forward in their journey.

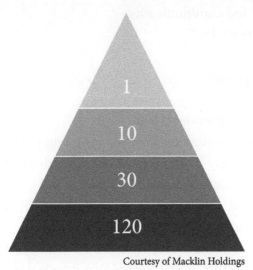

Courtesy of Macklin Holdings

This simple pyramid of 1, 10, 30 and 120 helps us understand how we all communicate, particularly in a business context.

- At the top of the pyramid is the service or product that offers one piece of information—one sentence answering: 'What is a detox?'
- One level down offers 10 pieces of information: '10 ways you can detox at home'
- One level beneath that offers 30 pieces of information: a fact sheet or a mini course
- The base of the pyramid offers 120 pieces of information, where you can get into peer-reviewed papers and more

extensive research: perhaps a full course or a workshop
We all have a '120 person' in our lives. You ask them a seemingly simple question, and they somehow give an in-depth and detailed breakdown of the topic just to arrive at what seems to be a fairly simple answer. What you thought would be a one-sentence answer becomes a fifteen-minute retelling of how we got there.

My teenagers, after they get home from school, are at the 1 level of focus and communication.

'How was your day?'

'Good.'

'What did you do?'

'Stuff.'

'How are your friends? Good.'

In a business context of what we are going to create, the top of the pyramid may be the topic itself: a hard-hitting sentence, or a small paragraph that is full of useful and easily digestible information that hooks people in and allows them to explore what may be under the surface.

Some of your clients may love the scientific-review level of data, but putting that in an ebook may not appeal to the masses.

Consider what level of information your ideal client would like to delve into and match that.

Take a moment to think, from your instincts, about the products or services you already offer:

- Where are you sharing more than you need?
- Where are you sharing too little?
- What are you excited to share more about?
- What topics or products are you happy to let go?

Constantly reassess the information you're sharing and how you can adjust it to make stronger connections, or to preserve your own energy and better serve your clients. That's how the magic can flow more freely!

Intentions and outcomes

It wouldn't be right to talk about the magic of business and reaching for the stars without also talking about the very tough times that can happen—when you act with integrity and in the best interests of a client, but still the outcome ends up hurting someone.

Even with your oath to do no harm, you can still harm people. It happens. Someone may have a reaction to something you give them for a condition they came to see you with. When this happens, learn from it, and make sure that everything gets back on track with your affected client.

The only time I have had a complaint made about me to the Consumer Commission was when a client ended up in hospital. This particular client had arrived in a fluster, admitted to mental health issues and long-term drug use, and filled out their new client form in a hurry. Through the consultation, I had a weird gut feeling that I should refer this client, but I kept on in the hope that I could help somehow.

I kept ticking along, confirming the new client form and double-checking their identification and current medications. Their complaint was their skin, and I noticed they didn't eat a lot of foods rich in vitamin A. So, I promptly recommended a probiotic fortified with vitamin A. Knowing that this has contraindications, I triple-checked whether they were on any other medications, and they insisted they weren't. Frustrated with all the questions, they hurriedly exited.

The next thing I knew, I was getting a call from the Consumer

Commission that this client had ended up in near liver failure in the local hospital. As more information was revealed, it was found that the client had 'forgotten' to mention her high-dose vitamin A pharmaceutical medication.

Although this was the worst situation I have found myself in, it hasn't been the only moment I've questioned whether I have helped someone. You can't predict the impact of your product or service on every human, physical or emotional. In the case of naturopathy, it could be a detox reaction, a niacin flush, or the emotional breakdown that comes before the breakthrough of changing the trajectory of your life.

No matter how well-meaning we may be, we can't always 'help' everyone. And sometimes a client will believe we've done more harm than good.

Since speaking to some friends in corporate, I have come to understand what is known in these circles as the 'querulent complainer'. In some big corporate businesses, there is a budget put aside for this specific type of situation. For most companies, there is an expectation that 1–3 per cent of people will complain.

When I got the call from the Consumer Commission, I had been in business five years and seen nearly seven thousand clients, and this was the only complaint I had to deal with. All I can say is, if you work from a place of integrity and keep coming back to the question of how you can best service your clients, you can rest assured that you did your best work for them.

Statistically, the likelihood of me receiving a complaint increases the more clients I see. As does the likelihood that some clients won't end up seeing the benefit in my services and products. Once I realised this, it was easier for me to continue with my intention of helping exactly who I am here to help.

Any complaints are an opportunity to tighten your processes and a reminder to trust your gut instincts next time.

"

You have
the capacity
to change
peoples lives
in ways you
can't even
imagine.

Chapter 10
Scale

 *Rule:* Don't stop until you have more

Fuel: Get clear on what success looks like to YOU, and aim for that

Getting fully booked is your goal, until it isn't. When you start out, you have all this enthusiasm and you work, work, work, work, work … until you drop. You realise that you have burnt yourself out. You can no longer show up as the best version of yourself. In pushing yourself to this point, you forget that you need to be your own healer.

Now, I do think that seeing your first hundred clients is an excellent starting point, because the process teaches you what it takes to acquire those clients, build rapport, and set timeframes. It also gives you experience in treating different conditions, so you can start to get the feel for what you might like to focus on.

I don't, however, think that 'more is more' is a sustainable way to run a business (unless you have a fully automated model). For entrepreneurs who have regular contact with all their clients, increasing your numbers needs to be done carefully—and from a mindset of enjoyment, not terror. Chasing more and more clients out of fear that you're not successful is a fast track to burnout.

So, how can we grow and scale in a more conscious and loving way?

Know the signs of burnout

I'll never forget sitting on the back step of my clinic at 8:00 am after dropping my kids to school one morning, experiencing my first panic attack. My focus was on a crack in the pavement; from it sprung a dandelion. There was no soil in the crack, but somehow this little medicinal weed—whose seeds most people blow to make wishes—had sprung up just there.

I was in one of the busiest years of my business ever; I was seeing record client numbers, and spending record hours on my business as well as *in* my business. And I was striving to create the next biggest thing.

At the same time, I couldn't bring myself to go to friends' parties or answer emails or text messages, especially if I had to interact in a way that would create more conversation. I definitely didn't have time for anything outside of work and home, or so I thought.

It wasn't until I found myself on that back step—staring at that crack, overwhelmed by the full day of clients to come, so consumed by not wanting to open the door—that I thought something might be wrong.

When you are putting in effort to create your business, run your practice and and achieve results for your clients, you are using a lot of energy. Sooner or later, burnout will happen. You are a better person and a better professional when you look after yourself.

As I've previously mentioned, I experienced burnout multiple times as a practitioner. Burnout is defined by long-term stress, which many of us have experienced during the pandemic years.

Challenge
Check in with yourself

Check in with yourself. Burnout can look like: pushing yourself to work harder and neglecting your own needs; skipping meals, working more hours over exercise and sleep; withdrawing from family friends and social situations; behavioural changes like impatience, blame and aggression; a feeling of detachment, worry or hopelessness. I wish it had been laid out as plainly and simply as this when I needed it most. If you notice you are nodding to a number of these, I invite you to open up and chat to a colleague, trusted advisor or health practitioner to create a plan to support you.

When to expand and build a team

Managing staff can be way harder than you think. But it's also incredibly rewarding. You learn all about making good people great and improving how you communicate.

Symptoms of needing to expand your team can include:

- Thinking about needing someone else on your team. This seems obvious, but often we ignore the nudge and let burnout creep in before we find someone to delegate to.
- Overwhelm, overtime, over budget—the feeling of having to do all. the. things! This leads to you doing nothing, or procrastinating so much that tasks take a lot longer than they need to.
- Identifying tasks that need specific skills you don't have, and don't have time to learn.

At a conference once, I listened to the CEO of one of the largest online fashion stores describe his biggest lessons in business. It was enlightening. He said the two biggest mistakes are staff related: one was not hiring for a culture fit, and the other was not letting go of someone quick enough.

I had both these issues in the first few years of my business—I don't believe they are exclusive to big business.

Finding a 'culture fit' means finding a staff member who aligns with your business's values and vision, and has the best intentions for your business and customers. I remember thinking I didn't have enough money to find someone who 'fit'; I was just looking for someone who could do the task I wanted. It wasn't until I was months down the track—correcting copy, changing the look and feel of content, and redoing work to be more in alignment—that I realised culture fit was so important.

This brings us to the second point: it took me months to let go of this team member who didn't fit. What we don't realise is that it is costing us time, money and even customers when we are keeping someone on who isn't right for the job.

Today, my team are integral to my business; they have the best intentions not just for my business, but also for my clients and me. We meet up monthly online, weekly and daily via our project management systems, and even for a retreat once a year to ensure we continue to be on the same track.

You may not find your team straight away, but don't give up looking for the right people. It's worth it.

Learn to say no

For me, one of the most powerful ways to remedy my burnout was learning to say no (yes, it's easier to say than to do).

When you're in your first few years of business, saying yes is important. The only way to learn to say no is by saying yes first.

When you say yes to everything, eventually you will hit that burnout stage I was talking about earlier. But this is how you learn your limits and create a business with healthy boundaries.

Learning to love the quiet(er) time

When we begin business, it can feel like fire. The survival mode that we are in—worried about where the money will come from and where the next client will come from, while excited to help people—doesn't usually match our skills as a businessperson. Similarly, over the life of our business, whenever we have an identity crisis, a pivot or a shift, these survival patterns kick back in again. We find ourselves in situations where the bills roll in, the launches don't go as we expect, and all the things we thought should work, don't.

Accepting the ebb and flow of business is part of enjoying the journey. I know, nobody loves a quiet patch, but this is when we can step back from the adrenaline, rest and recover, and look forward to bigger things happening in the future.

You'll never know it all (and that's ok)

I used to stress about a client coming in one day with a health issue that I wouldn't recognise or know much about. I learned over the years that it's okay to not know everything. There are sources you can turn to on just about anything. There is no shame in saying to your client, 'I am going to research this and will get back to you.'

I generally have my two favourite textbooks on the desk and we reference them together. I feel like this is an empowering tool that subconsciously gives clients permission to research for themselves in recommended ways (rather than using good old Dr Google).

Vulnerability is powerful

Show it. Show your flaws; they are part of what you are: human. Sharing your experiences gives your clients the impetus to do the same.

I remember a client coming in for help with mastitis, teary-eyed and sleep deprived. I could have easily imparted knowledge about bacterial infections in the mammary glands and milk ducts, but when I shared my experience of utter desperation to spend time with my mum while going through my third bout of mastitis, she was so relieved to hear she wasn't alone.

You will forget people

You will forget people's names, their problems, their jobs, what they previously ordered from your business. And, it's okay. When you see hundreds of people a year or sell hundreds or thousands of products, it's a tall order to remember everyone's names and details. Don't beat yourself up about it.

When I was a bartender in Soho, London, I prided myself on knowing all the regulars' names and drinks; it was something that connected me to everyone there. When I got a second job at the University College London pathology department during the day, I found that there was less room in my brain, so names started to disappear. But I still managed to pour the right drinks for the right faces at my pub job.

Years later, back home in Australia, as my clinic grew, I would be walking through my local farmers' market and random people would come up to say hello. I would remember they had a thyroid issue or regular diarrhoea, but their names escaped me.

I felt really down on myself when it first started happening, as I pride myself on the connections I make.

But as time goes on, you realise that it's a numbers game and you are human. There is no point in beating yourself up about it.

We are all just winging it

Even those you look up to in the field are all just winging it. We are all in the same boat, doing the best we can with the tools we have.

In 2014, when I ran my first teleseminar, I reached out to my top twelve naturopathic heroes and asked if I could interview them about life and business. Ten said yes.

Ever since then, their answers have stuck with me.

- A practitioner with a multi-million-dollar practice, whose products impact thousands of people, attributed his success firstly to a series of coincidences (having found himself in front of the right people, at the right time), and secondly to trial and error.
- An award-winning author and practitioner admitted it took her years to write her book. But when it finally came out, it was sold and translated into so many different languages.
- I spoke to the incredible wellness educator Petrea King about her residential programs for those experiencing chronic conditions. She mentioned that, if it weren't for the timing of a television interview, Quest for Life residential programs would have closed their doors in mere weeks.

Each of these three individuals had a personal story of juggling all of this with family dynamics, kids, health issues and life changes.

We are all humans, just winging it.

Remember when you found out our parents weren't the be-all and end-all? They were humans making mistakes! It's true of the entrepreneurs and role models you look up to as well.

Chapter 11
Acknowledge and Renew

 **Rule:** Hustle and keep going no matter what

Fuel: Nature has it right: there is a reason and a season for it all

I know what it takes to not only make the commitment, but follow it through week after week. And, I know what it's like to move on to the next little thing on your to-do list and completely forget—or not acknowledge—how far you've come.

We need to create a habit of celebrating little wins and milestones. For me, there are three parts to doing that.

- We need to **acknowledge**—this is something that we don't prioritise enough as practitioners in business.
- We need to **review** and measure.
- Lastly, we need to **renew**—what does it look like to really take care of yourself so that you're ready for the next cycle in your business?

Often, we're very good at acknowledging others, but not so great at acknowledging ourselves. I want you to get in your little time machine and think back to when you first started reading this book or had an idea for your business or new career.

What were you like? What were you thinking about? What did you want to achieve?

Now is your opportunity to take every single thing that you actually did and give yourself a gold star—give yourself the acknowledgement you deserve.

It's amazing how far you've come and it's really, really important that you celebrate and renew. Just as the seasons go from one to the next, it's time to close down this chapter, renew yourself and get ready for the next season in your business.

What does renewal look like for you? We're so good at giving self-help and self-care tips to all of our clients, but when it comes to ourselves—sometimes it can be a little harder to do. What puts you in the best position possible to look after and nourish yourself, especially when heading into the next phase of your business?

Challenge
Reflect and renew YOU

It's time to look in the mirror, reflect, and take the time to renew.

Your challenge is to write down all of the places or activities that make you feel your best, and then pick an activity you love to do or a place you love to visit. This is your time to go and run yourself a bath, or make a cuppa with the nice herbal tea. Use that massage voucher or go get your hair done.

You need to celebrate in a way that renews you, and it's time to celebrate you *now*.

Review and finish strong

To finish strong, we need to go through a review: review where you were at when you first picked up this book or started your business. Review where you've adjusted your focus (since you've learnt that where attention goes, energy flows!).

The exact areas that you review will be personal, but here are some jumping-off points to get you started:

- Where have you implemented those boundaries and time schedules?
- How are you spending your time now?
- What systems have you signed up for or put into place?
- How are these systems making your life easier?
- How is your booking system?
- Where have you automated?
- Have you put out a newsletter or a blog post?
- What does your social media page look like?
- Do you have consistent posts?
- Are you building connections?
- Have you started using multiple social media platforms?
- Have you been repurposing your content?
- Are you keeping in mind that it costs seventy per cent less time and money to re-engage clients than it does to find new ones?

Now consider where you want to be in the near future. Pull out your flight plan again—what is tracking along? What areas need more attention? Since it is a long-term plan, are you on track to hit three- or six-month goals? Have you been taking inspired action?

Whenever you feel like you might not be moving ahead with

your business (and you're in a season where you have the energy to scale and move forward), there are some questions you can turn to! Bookmark this page and keep it on hand for when you need it.

- **Attitude.** Where have you adjusted your attitude, knowing that it affects your behaviour and the final outcome? Are you still checking in with your concerns, criticisms and complaints? Are you taking action on clearing these?

- **Value.** Did you rediscover your value and how others perceive you? And how are you leveraging your value through people, referrals, connections and systems? Who are your referral partners, and when was the last time you connected with them? Are there some personal trainers, hairdressers, beauticians or GPs in the mix? If not, book in that conversation.

- **Connection.** Have you become clearer on the fact that it doesn't matter if we operate business-to-corporate, business-to-business or business-to-consumer; we always need to focus on the human-to-human connection? What stories have you been using from your story bank in order to build those connections? Which ones really resonate with people? Do your stories follow the high-low-high structure? And have you remembered to detach from the outcome when having those sales conversations?

- **Procrastination.** What about those frogs, have they been eaten? Are they on the breakfast menu each day? Which tasks are the most urgent and consequential and will move you further along?

- **Celebration.** How important it is to come full circle and celebrate what has actually been happening for us. We talked about gratitude and how that invites flow in because we need to acknowledge the goodness that has been happening in our lives. We also took a moment for self-care—we've even scheduled self-care in so that it doesn't fall by the wayside.

Remember, the point is to make our business unrestricted and sustainable—so that, as we run this marathon, we're able to not only nourish our business, but also nourish ourselves so that we can truly show up in our business.

I want you to finish strong. All the elements in this book build upon each other and come together to create a flow of ideal clients, business, creativity and cash.

What have you not actioned yet that called to you as you read this chapter? I'm inviting you to get through that last five per cent in order to really get the full benefit of this book. Commit yourself so that you can help a lot more people, and be financially rewarded for the amazing work that you do.

You are exactly where you need to be

Don't compare yourself to anyone else's journey. You are walking your own path. You are learning what you need to learn, at the pace you need to learn it.

We all have these thoughts and feelings. Stay in your own lane. Every single moment is either an incredible lesson or an amazing experience, and you need them both. You can't just take all the good things and not acknowledge the bad stuff. It's all part and parcel.

"

You are
exactly where
you need
to be.

Chapter 12
Loving Life and Letting Go

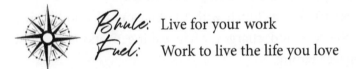

Rule: Live for your work

Fuel: Work to live the life you love

Nearly losing the love of my life taught me to focus on the important things in life, as well as the power of 'automate, delegate and eliminate'.

It was October 2018. Heading towards the end of one of my biggest years yet, Murray and I decided to take our annual family trip to New Zealand. A few years prior, we had committed to working towards a goal of going on four trips a year—one for our business, one for ourselves, one as a couple and one as a family.

This particular year, my business boomed. This involved thirty flights and 71,638 km of flying away from home, touring Australia and New Zealand; running retreats across Indonesia and the Pacific Islands; and attending conferences in New York and Canada. Murray's business had also expanded and he had taken a similar amount of time away from home, so we were all looking forward to the quality time together.

The air in Wanaka still had a crispness, even though the ski town hadn't had snow in months. We decided to hire mountain bikes for us and our three kids for the day, and complete a bike tour along the river together. We had regular stops for photos of us all in helmets, laughing along the alpine river. We egged one another on to keep going and finish together.

The following day was our last full day, and Murray and our sixteen-year-old decided they wanted to make the most of the last morning by hiring the bikes one last time. I took the rest of the family for an early morning walk around the nearby lake to see the famous tree within it—another photo-op and an incredible spot to skip stones before meeting for lunch. It was just past 10:30 am when my phone buzzed: a call from Murray.

They weren't due to finish with the bikes until midday, and he hated the fees and charges when calling overseas. I knew something was wrong.

'I've fallen off the bike and I think I've done something to my arm,' Murray said. 'I might have broken it—it hurts so bad.'

'Where are you?' I demanded, already running up the street back towards our hire car, mouthing to my eldest to look after our little one and head back to the hotel.

'I don't know … somewhere in the forest,' Murray said. 'I went headfirst into a tree, smashed my helmet and I can't get comfortable. I feel really sick. I'm walking around in circles like our dog … but my arm is so painful.'

'Okay, stay where you are. I'll come and get you. Is Noah there?'

Having recently done my required first aid refresher for work, all signs were pointing to a spinal injury and I didn't want him to move.

'Yeah,' he said. 'Noah is here. We are going to ride out of the forest—'

Click. He hung up.

I got to the car and, only knowing the general direction of the forest they were riding in, began driving.

It was a Sunday. I didn't know the emergency services numbers, and couldn't tell them where to go even if I did, so I just drove.

I know it sounds whacky, but I followed my intuition, looking for signs saying 'Beacon Point Road' or 'Clearview Street'. Sure enough, when they finally answered my call, I was less than one hundred metres away. Murray was lying flat on his back, gripping his right arm, while Noah looked after the bikes.

As I went to get Murray up into the car, his hands shot straight to the back of his neck and he said, 'I think I'm going to be sick.' My first aid brain knew these were not good signs, but I also knew I didn't want this to define my kids' lives. Stabilising Murray with blankets and towels, Noah and I had some laughs about how it all happened, then I dropped Noah and the bikes off on my way to the nearest medical centre (there is no hospital in Wanaka).

By this time, I was near certain Murray had a spinal injury that was radiating down his arm. Although the X-ray was not sensitive enough to pick it up, the local medical staff put him in a neck brace and asked if I wanted to wait the six hours for an ambulance or drive the ninety minutes to get a CT scan.

They assured me that the blankets and towels with the neck brace were likely more comfortable than and just as safe as the ambulance.

As I drove through mining gorges to the nearest country hospital, in a hired mini-van, with no reception and my love lying next to me in so much pain, I pondered how quickly things can change.

Sure enough, the CT scan showed a fracture of the C3 and C4 vertebrae, and we had to stay overnight to stabilise the fracture and the pain medications. The country hospital didn't allow visitors overnight and I found myself in planning mode on the drive back to the hotel. Our flights were due out the following evening, and I knew the kids needed to see their dad before leaving, and that I'd have to stay.

I also knew that I didn't want this moment to define what was an epic holiday, so I stayed up well past midnight planning a visit to the lavender farm, an alpaca morning tea and fruit picking for the kids just before the hospital. We also found the best doughnuts in Queenstown to round off the trip before they got on the plane home.

There were laughs, there were tears, there were memories made and a lot of love. There was also a mastermind group call on my phone from the hospital courtyard for my ongoing program, and messages with my virtual assistant to ensure my day-to-day was being looked after while I changed flights and looked at options for insurance and medical travel plans.

That evening, I jumped up on Murray's hospital bed and snuggled into his chest. This is my spot. My home. With one leg over his body, I snuggled under his arm and listened to his heartbeat.

He said, 'The doctor came in today and mentioned it would have only been a matter of millimetres and this "stable" fracture would have severed everything from my neck down and stopped my breathing.'

We were in New Zealand another five days. Knowing Murray was stable, I got to truly try out my 'work from wherever' catchcry and my goal of running my business from my phone. I had all my emails automated, my inbox and socials delegated, non-essentials eliminated, and all that was left was my weekly group calls. The relief I felt to have the space for this—with the money still appearing in the business account from passive income and payment plans—left me the energy I needed to fill out insurance forms and focus on getting Murray home for the treatment he needed.

Only twenty-four hours after we returned home, Murray had the surgery he needed for a titanium cage to stabilise his C3 and C4, and walked out of the hospital.

A matter of weeks later, we were both in Bali teaching a retreat of fifty people, doing all the things we love together.

Since the pandemic, many of us have experienced a stripping back to what's important. At the time of writing this, we are in the midst of what many are calling 'the great resignation'. Globally, there is a shift to create a life that works for us, rather than working for a life.

My call to action is: you don't have to wait until you nearly lose something to make big changes or to step into your power.

Set up your life now so that it supports the best version of you, your business and your family.

For entrepreneurs and anyone ready to impact the world by learning to harness creative power in an authentic way: learn to trust your calling, let go of being controlled by money, and step into being the amazing leader you're meant to be.

Avoiding the guru complex

If you're positioning yourself as an expert who people can't live without, it changes the dynamic of the relationship between you and your client. It puts them in a position of being the one who needs to be fixed—a problem to be solved. It disempowers people and makes them feel like they are broken.

Our job as a practitioner (or any service-offering entrepreneur) is to create a space where the person can heal their body and feel empowered.

My ego ran wild for a stint when I was creating my first e-course; if you look back at the videos from this era, you'd think, *Wow, she's a woman on a mission with scary intensity.* At the time,

I made myself an expert in adrenal fatigue and looked for all the broken stress-hormone pathways I could find within my clients so I could fix them.

I went away on a conference and as I walked across the road to lunch, although I was in New York with some of the most inspiring entrepreneurial minds, I answered text messages and emails from clients asking about foods they were eating or not eating, if supplements they had seen on an evening news program could be more appropriate than something I had prescribed, and why I hadn't emailed back immediately since their last message.

I had taught these clients that I was the sole source of the information and guidance that they needed, and that they had no ability whatsoever to make decisions about their own bodies in my absence. Their own bodies!

It was in this moment that the impact of my actions became clear. If I continued to be the one source of all my clients' answers, then I would continue to rob them of their power to find their own answers, their sovereignty over their body and their real healing capacity.

There is a magic when you see a client come to their own aha moment; when they come in and tell you their journey of getting through a tough spot, or how they shared their insights with a loved one. There is also a certain magic that comes with having an entire weekend uninterrupted by client text messages or late-night emails.

Resources, referrals, and reminders about how to best get in contact are so much more empowering for your clients than you being a 'guru'.

"

BE it,
until you
SEE it.

Recap:
Your unrestricted life

As I come to the end of writing this book, it's time for me to take on board my own advice. Because there is nothing more restricted than clinging to a project and fearing letting it go. There comes a time in all our businesses when we have to take a leap, release our grip and trust that we've done enough—and that what we have to offer will land with the people who need it right now.

As the founder of the Natupreneur Movement, it was my mission to amplify the value of practitioners so that they can create real change for their clients. I know this book will reach further and wider than I had dreamed for that movement, because I have given it the space and freedom to grow into everything it needs to be.

And now it's over to you!

As I stated at the start of this book, this is your chance to build a business with an authentic, grounding and evolving mindset that supports the world and its healing. We can ALL be natupreneurs, and the planet and everyone on it needs us more than ever.

So, my call to action is for you to use this book as a guide and dip back into it whenever you need to feel anchored; use it as a reminder to flow with the seasons of your business, rest when you need to, and trust the next stage of your growth when it calls you.

I hope you can put the systems in place to support every stage of your business and also allow yourself the space to dream big and change your plans when you need to. More importantly, in this slightly chaotic world, I want you to trust you're exactly where you need to be.

An unrestricted mindset will create an unrestricted business— the kind of business that feels good and thrives.

Afterword

Flying high

I had been learning to fly helicopters on and off for about two years—originally to combat my adrenal fatigue and an identity crisis I had when I became a mother, wife and business owner in a short period of time.

When I ran my clinic, I used to tell my burnt-out clients that one of the most powerful things they could do was remember the things that brought them joy. I would suggest that they write down five things that brought them joy when they were younger, or things they wish they had done but never got around to. And, just like my clients, I had forgotten what these things were in the midst of work and family, family and work.

Fast forward to two years later, and I'd sat six theory exams for my commercial pilot's license. I had forty hours of flying under my belt with my instructors, in two different aircraft, and it was about this time that most expect to fly solo.

Flying solo means going without an instructor, at the controls of a multi-million-dollar flying machine, when all manner of things that you have just learnt about and been theoretically examined on can go drastically wrong.

I knew the risk was low; the systems, processes and hardware are tested and maintained. You have every piece of evidence you need that flying solo is not only possible, but actually the next logical step.

There is a term we use in the flying world: pilot in command or PIC.

In my logbook, which trainee pilots have to complete, all

my flights until this point had the initials of my instructors in the PIC column. As trainees, we practise saying 'I have control.' Then the other person in the aircraft responds with 'You have control' to confirm.

I had always, however, still deferred to the other person in the aircraft.

I visualised myself with a PIC cap on, in full control of the aircraft, confident, decisive, safe, secure and having fun. My new question was: who do I need to BE in order to be the person in control?

Three days later, with my imaginary PIC cap imbuing me with confidence, I got in the chopper with my instructor and we flew to our practice airfield. And what do you know? My instructor promptly hopped out of the aircraft and said, 'Today's the day. You are ready. I'll see you back here after three circuits.'

I completed those circuits with all the confidence and fun that I had hoped for and loved every second.

As I picked up my instructor, with utter joy I said, 'I have control.'

And he responded, 'You have control.'

Seemingly, for the first time in years, I truly was in control of my life. Looking back on my Instagram photos of that time, you can see that within the space of three days, I go from distraught tears, deferring to the instructors, to total elation hugging the helicopter.

Where in your life might you be handing over control to other people?

I find that many new business owners act as though they have a hobby rather than a business: whether it is handing over control in their mind to their partner or someone in their past who they believe knows more than them about business, or just making themselves smaller than they need to be. They hand over control for as long as they can, until something breaks. It's a moment where all the things that they were doing before stop working altogether.

Often, I refer to this as the breakdown before the breakthrough. This happens when we are squashed so far up against our old comfort zones that there is no room for anything else; the old version of us has to crumble to allow space for the current version of us to break through to a new comfort zone. This is generally not a comfortable process, but the gold is in finding comfort in the uncomfortable—the biggest signpost of growth occurring.

If I know anything about business, it's that it is one of the biggest personal growth journeys you can go on.

Remember a time in your life that you would consider a breakdown moment: one of the biggest challenges you have been through. Now take a moment to consider the breakthrough: what was the lesson you took from it?

If nothing else, you can get through the tough times; you've done it before. The same goes for the tough times in your business.

Lastly, sometimes in the most challenging moments of doing something new or having something change, all the 'doing' in the world doesn't change things. Sometimes it helps to ponder the question: Who do I need to BE in order to DO or HAVE this?

Just as I did with the PIC, who could you borrow the traits of to get through this shift you require? I have done this with people I know and admire, public figures alive and dead—even fictional characters like Wonder Woman.

The new adage of 'be it until you see it' applies here.

Who do I need to BE in order to DO or HAVE this?

As you come to the end of this book, I want to leave you with something to consider: what you believe, you can conceive.

I choose to believe in an unrestricted life.

I believe we all have a choice.

I believe in the thrill of the first time, so much so that beginning new things has become a sport.

I believe in the power of the pack; we can't do it alone and nothing survives in a vacuum.

I believe in the power of nature; her presence and cycles have given harmony and rhythm to the world for billions of years. I believe in the limitless potential of every single human, cell and atom. When we get down to it, it's all pure energy.

I believe in the unrestricted life: looking beyond the horizon for possibilities not yet realised.

I believe in the ripple effect of travel through time and space; I believe that the trajectory of one's life can change through a serendipitous conversation with a stranger.

I believe entrepreneurship has changed the game and allowed all of us access to create our own destinies. I believe there is always a way; we just have to figure it out.

I believe that just like the moon, we go through phases, only to become more whole again. I believe we all have gifts and talents, and the more we stay true to them, the more flow we have in life.

I believe things that tire us or inspire us are signposts with which to choose our own adventure. (And I choose inspiration every time.)

I believe where your attention goes, energy flows. I believe freedom can be found when you truly commit. I believe structure enables flexibility.

I believe a pair of thongs can be appropriate to climb a mountain.

I believe in the healing power of nature … and a hug and a listening ear.

I believe the world would be a better place if we all just gave a shit. I believe that things break in order to become stronger in the long run.

I believe hidden gems are found when you stop looking. I believe that nuggets of gold can be found in any situation or conversation, if you dare to look.

I believe there is beauty in the small things. I believe that Converse are a timeless classic and one pair can take you all around the globe.

As cliché as it is, I believe a journey doesn't begin until you take the first step. I believe too much time is wasted worrying about why things can't be done, when there is far more power in focusing on what can be done.

I believe living an unrestricted life means embracing change, but being unmoved by outside forces, and being the calmest person in the room, with limitless possibilities available.

It's not just staying in your own lane, but ignoring that there are any lanes in the first place; it's building your own roller-coaster or flying a helicopter.

I believe in living an *unrestricted life*.

I believe you can access all of the above—and more!

Acknowledgements

For those I love: Murray, Mia, Noah and Elliot—for always making memories together.

For my ancestors: my mum, my dad, my sister Melita, and my lineage that had the courage to go on their own adventures and instil that sense of adventure in me.

For the original custodians of the land on which I work and live, the Awabakal people. I acknowledge their elders, past, present and emerging and their ongoing custodianship of country.

For friendship and support: Naomes, Denise, Vari, Hayley, Ally, Kira—for having my back.

For your teachings and inspiration: Amber, Hen and Kate, Carrie-Anne Moss, Roger Hamilton, Jonathan Fields, Paul Macklin, Marie Forleo, Hiro Boga—we stand on the shoulders of giants.

For helping me make this book a reality: Natasha, Amy, Georgia—I've learned so much.

For my community: health seekers, health providers, and businesses committed to the health of the planet, you are more powerful than you know.

About the author

TAMMY GUEST

Tammy Guest takes people on adventures and reminds them of how to live. She spent a career working in cancer wards and studying life and death, and it shaped the way she teaches today; she reminds us of how unique and precious we are, and how important it is to shake things up.

Tammy founded the Natupreneur Movement and hosts huge events around the country. She runs retreats both online and in person on leadership, business and freedom, with her Unrestricted retreat pairing powerfully with this book.

Tammy is also a mother, step-mother, wife, student helicopter pilot and artist.

Unrestricted is Tammy's second book, offering practical new wisdoms that beautifully complement the teachings of her 2016 title *Freedom from Fatigue*.

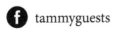 tammyguests    @tammyguests

www.tammyguest.com

Printed in Australia
AUHW020840020822
367050AU00003B/3

9 780645 011388